Leadership is a carefully honed set of skills and behaviors. As such, personal backgrounds, experiences, families, communities, spirituality, and ethics all contribute to the identity of a leader. In *Leadership Wisdom for All Generations*, Jennifer Wimbish pulls back the curtain on the personal journey which chiseled her into an effective leader. In short vignettes—from her childhood in the segregated South to her presidency at a diverse community college—Dr. Wimbish shares poignant insights from her past which grounded and shaped her character and leadership. Aspiring leaders will find this text motivating and full of practical wisdom. Experienced leaders will nod in shared understanding of many of the points made and challenges faced. Indeed, women of all generations, faiths, races, and ethnicities will find strength in the mirror of straightforward guidance Dr. Wimbish holds before us.

—Dr. Marilyn J. Amey
Professor of Educational Administration and
Department Chair at Michigan State University
Co-Author of *Beginning Your Journey: A Guide for
New Professionals in Student Affairs*

Beautifully presented as an autobiographical journey through the phases of life, *Leadership Wisdom for All Generations* will help anyone lead and mentor with dignity and effectiveness—even if accosted by relentless racial and social injustice. Dr. Wimbish's seamless weaving of stories and strategy also helps us as parents, friends, spouses, neighbors, siblings and, in fact, as humans. Anyone seeking to makes positive contributions in the lives of others will relish the upbeat and powerful lessons in this book.

—Bea Boccalandro
President of VeraWorks and author of *The Job Purposing Blog*
Teacher of corporate community involvement at
Georgetown University

Leadership Wisdom for All Generations is both simple and insightful. Dr. Wimbish manages to express her message in a compelling fashion that is reminiscent of listening to one's own family. This book stays true to its title by offering aphorisms which will resonate with anyone—regardless of age.

—Veronica Carleton
Undergraduate student at St. Edward's University, Class of 2020

As leaders, it is important that we all take time to intentionally learn and glean from the wisdom of individuals whom we respect. Dr. Wimbish offers a wealth of leadership lessons in her book and uses a faith perspective to do so. More specifically, she highlights the need for leaders to trust God and listen for His voice. I assure you these are nuggets of wisdom that all leaders should subscribe to as they endeavor to have a dynamic influence. We cannot lead on our own; we need heavenly guidance.

—Rev. Bryan L. Carter
Senior Pastor of Concord Church in Dallas, TX
Lead for Harmony Community Development Corporation

When we were students at Hampton University, Jennifer Butler Wimbish always seemed wise beyond her years. It was a treat for our circle of friends to listen to what the special people in her life had taught her. Now, thank God, she has written a book to share her wisdom, knowledge, and experiences. Young people, parents, and grandparents will be inspired and motivated as they turn the pages and take this amazing journey with the author.

—Joyce Carter-Ball, J. D.
Tennessee Administrative Law Judge
Author, *Planted by The Waters* and *As Soft as Cotton*

Dr. Jennifer Wimbish's outstanding career in education is widely respected by all of us who have led educational institutions. She is a leader among leaders. As a true servant leader, Dr. Wimbish has now written this book in order to help all of us know and understand how to better lead and serve. This excellent book unites leadership and biblical principles in ways that encourage leaders to live true to their values.

—Dr. Gary Cook
Chancellor Emeritus of Dallas Baptist University
Chair of Baylor Medical School

Leadership Wisdom for All Generations invites us to take a journey, and in doing so, to also remember our own upbringings, shrouded in sage advice from our parents, community leaders, and a belief in someone greater than ourselves. In this book, Dr. Jennifer Wimbish openly shares how her personal and professional experiences helped frame her both as an individual and an educational leader. She reminds us that lessons learned and personal experiences help us to act and think differently—not just to survive, but to thrive in this changing world. This book permits us to travel from one place to the next and encourages us to remember from whence we came and how far we can go. Enjoy your journey!

—**Dr. Rufus Glasper**
President and CEO of League for Innovation
Chancellor Emeritus, Maricopa Community Colleges

In her book, *Leadership Wisdom for All Generations*, Dr. Wimbish provides leadership principles that are valuable, life-changing, and that challenge all to lead with integrity. Through telling her story, she has done what it is so important for each generation to do—engage in generational transformation. Her written accounts of lessons from the past serve us well today. Her personal journey and voice on leadership is one that inspires, and it results in a must-read book for every current and emerging leader.

—**Dr. Harry Robinson, Jr**.
CEO and President of the African American
Museum in Dallas, Texas

Dr. Jennifer Wimbish has written a must-read for all parents, educators, and advocates for youth empowerment. This is an eloquent and honest account of the impact that adults leave upon the lives of children. It serves as a guide for self-reflection and raises awareness of self-worth, purposeful living, and the importance of meaningful interactions for both youth and adults.

—**Rickenya Sisk**
Parent, Educator, Youth Mentor

Jennifer Wimbish's book provides a profoundly inspiring example of a leader's reflective practice. As the challenges facing higher education and society have escalated, there is heightened demand for wise leaders with strong character. Wisdom and character can be developed. Through a revealing portrait of her journey as a leader, the author provides important guidance to others who must learn and grow from these experiences. Leadership development programs will benefit from this introspective, value-laden approach to doing the important work as leaders in any sectors—our communities, our organizations, or our colleges. At a time when many have lost faith in our institutions, this read will restore your faith in what is possible while serving others. *Leadership Wisdom for All Generations* also provides specific guidance for becoming this kind of much-needed leader.

—Dr. Roberta C. Teahen
Director of Doctorate in Community College
Leadership at Ferris State University
Associate Provost for Accreditation, Assessment,
Compliance, and Evaluation at Ferris State University

LEADERSHIP WISDOM FOR ALL GENERATIONS

UNIQUE INSIGHTS FROM AUTHENTIC LEADERS

BY JENNIFER WIMBISH, PH.D.

ISBNs

Hardback
978-1-64184-957-9

Softcover
978-1-64184-958-6

Ebook
978-1-64184-959-3

Dedication

I would like to dedicate this book to my husband, son, and daughter-in-law, Michael, Michael, Jr., and Jesslynn Wimbish, all of whom have supported me during the journey towards my completion of the book. I also dedicate this work to granddaughters, Kailynn, Jordynn, Kendall and Mikayla.

I would also like to dedicate this book to my father, the late Louis Grant Butler, and my mother, Jenell Butler, who instilled in me a love for God, family, and service to others. Additionally, I dedicate the book to a loving brother, Steven Grant Butler.

Honoring Wise, Authentic, Mentors

Bessie Auls, Rev. Harold Branch, Dr. Patsy Fulton-Calkins, Naomi Chase, Dorothy Drinkard, Rev. John Dudley, Annette Flowers, Marjorie Green, Dr. Asa Hilliard, Seretha Hilliard, Dr. Thomas Hilliard, Dr. Dianne Horton, Dr. Don Lamb, Mattie Martin, Lavernis Royal, Dr. Abel Sykes, Rev. John Tatum, Dr. Carolyn Williams, Ovelle Williams, and Dr. Ronald Wright.

Special Thanks

Pamela Ice, Ellen Benson, Rosalyn Story, and Jennie Weber, who provided guidance and valuable insights during the journey towards completing this project.

Thanks also to Editors

Jennifer Carson

Kristin Denise Rowe
Doctoral Candidate
African American and African Studies (AAAS)
Michigan State University, East Lansing, MI

for their patience, insightful answers to my questions, editing and revisions that enhanced the book.

FOREWORD

I am honored and humbled to contribute to *Leadership Wisdom for All Generations* written by Dr. Jennifer Wimbish, president emeritus of Cedar Valley College of the Dallas Community College District. She is a presidential colleague; my sister in Delta Sigma Theta Sorority, Incorporated; my friend; and—in ways too numerous to detail—my mentor in my personal and professional paths to serenity and leadership. Dr. Wimbish is a trailblazer, paving the way for so many leaders and women of color to see and grasp opportunities for their own career trajectories, while accepting the mantle and responsibility of senior roles in higher education.

She is a spiritual guide for all who understand the power of faith and the enduring belief in a God who can do all things. She is a warrior, having dedicated her life and her work to uplift marginalized and underrepresented populations of women and men of color, as students and professionals, throughout all sectors of education.

This book, in each of its parts and chapters, details what Dr. Wimbish learned through teachings and conversations at the feet of her family and other elders in the communities where she lived and worked. It speaks to the "symphonies" of life and the synchronization of amazing high notes, as well as the timbre of the challenging low tones throughout her career. It is both philosophical and practical, offering advice and counsel through the sharing of stories and circumstances. There is an unspoken yet clearly delineated commitment to diversity, inclusion, change, and growth, requiring the reader to embrace the lessons learned and bask in the possibilities of application to his or her own life.

Ultimately, this book reveals the humanity and humility of Dr. Jennifer Wimbish, a woman of faith, followship, and fidelity, who adheres to a strong set of principles and values from her earliest beginnings to the present. The "Early Years" lead the reader to comprehend the "why" behind her voice and her actions in the latter years. It is a story of life and legacy.

In Jeremiah 29:11, we read "For I know the plans I have for you," declares the Lord, "plans to prosper you and not harm you, plans to give you hope and a future." Dr. Wimbish's life is one of success and significance, fueled by an unwavering commitment to teach and learn, concurrently. For this, she has prospered mightily.

With pride,
Dr. Charlene Mickens Dukes, President
Prince George's Community College

CONTENTS

PART THREE: LEGACY

INTRODUCTION

Today, I am more sure than ever that I stand on the shoulders of great leaders and a mighty God who have provided direction and special insight for my life. Upon reflection, great individuals and mentors stand out clearly in the landscape of my life. They include family, friends, teachers, pastors, colleagues, and community leaders, who have each played a vital role in my story. In the words of one aunt who significantly impacted me, "I am a part of all those who I have met that took the time to share their lives with me and/or mentored me." I will be forever grateful to God and the dynamic individuals He placed in my life, whose words I present to you in this book.

Following Christ intentionally since the age of six has brought divine direction and knowledge to my life, crafted by the Master. I have come to understand that life is not an accident. That is, we are placed in unique locations with specific people and circumstances at designated times. Our lives are like symphonies, carefully composed by the marvelous Master. Each life is a melody invented precisely for our personal journey through life—for our greater joy and our deeper understanding. Truly, as the Bible teaches, "All things work together for the good of those that love the Lord" (Romans 8:28).

Looking back on the various phases of my life, I hear specific words of wisdom from voices along the journey. I recall sage comments, enlightening experiences, and astute observations from great leaders who impacted my life for the better. Furthermore, at every stage of life, words of wisdom have been inspired by God's written word, His voice, and His people, whom He strategically placed in my path to encourage and edify me. I often hear the echoes of these wise words concerning the many roles I play in life. Throughout the telling of this book, I am a daughter, student, teacher, employee, supervisor, wife, mother, community leader, and finally the president of a community college. Professionally, I have served as a faculty member, counselor, dean, and provost in the community college before becoming a president. At every point, I have received wisdom and guidance from amazing people.

I begin this book as a mentee and end as a mentor who continues to learn. In each phase, however, I am—above all— a follower of Christ, knowing His evident hand is on my life in each period. Now in retirement, new roles include being a grandmother, Cedar Valley College President Emeritus, and a Christian matriarch. From where I sit now, I feel profoundly moved to share these written words of wisdom, not only to honor those who mentored me, but also to provide pivotal instructions for future generations to consider. Hours of reflection have caused me to realize that it often took years for me to truly grasp what these words of wisdom meant. Only through time and circumstance did learning truly occur. Now, I offer these words to others, so that they may apply them to their own journeys and experience their own revelations.

In this book, I share only those words of wisdom applied for many years and found to be effective tools for productive and successful living. There have been times that I did not follow the advice presented in these pages, and I have deeply regretted the times I did not do so. Each chapter begins with information about my life, somewhat of an autobiography, designed to provide background and a better understanding of my worldview. This is, indeed, my story connected to a rich legacy, a history presented here for others to meditate on as a part of their own personal growth. Often, words of wisdom came from hours of discussion with individuals who were model leaders. I considered them models, because their words were so clearly consistent with their actions. More times than not, these leaders did more than offer words of advice on difficult decisions; they also became active mentors, walking me through life's greatest challenges. Some words of wisdom represent my observations of individuals whom I admired more from a distance, but whose examples shined a light on treasured truths and insights. I have used the principles these men and women presented to develop a system for thinking and solving problems, often leading to positive life-altering results.

Specific stories and experiences often accompanied these valuable words of wisdom, raising me to a greater level of understanding. Such stories and illustrations follow important points after the autobiography in each chapter. In contrast, other words and phrase were simply spoken—sometimes once and sometimes repeatedly. These are highlighted in a sidebar at the end of each chapter entitled *"Echoes . . ."* These small pieces of advice often lingered in my mind, bringing serious reflection and deep thought about how such ideas applied to my own life. My goal in recording these words is for you to consider them in a similar manner, thus gaining insights to help you solve problems and attain your goals.

While I could have also written about the mistakes and misguided advice that has undoubtedly been part of the learning process, I have instead decided to share only those words of wisdom that represent, for me, the very best. I end this publication with my own words of wisdom, developed from personal life experiences. I am sure that they come deep from within my soul and build on the lessons presented by others. In this way, I join the dialogue initiated by others, allowing me to contribute to the conversation and leave a legacy for future generations. **If you discover but one concept that assists you with productive citizenship and living, then I have accomplished my goal. Enjoy.**

HOW TO USE THIS BOOK

IF YOU ARE A . . .	THEN FOCUS ON . . .
Parent or Teacher	Chapters 1-3
Youth or Student	Chapters 1-4
Leader	Chapters 4-7 and 9
Working Mother	Chapters 1-3 and 8

PART ONE

CHARACTER

CHAPTER ONE

THE EARLY YEARS

Children are born into this world with unique and diverse learning characteristics, capabilities, potentialities, desires, urges, needs and . . . children [must] be surrounded by people who love and care for them and who understand that the environment children are placed in contributes to their future success or failure in life.

—Seretha Hilliard[1]

The community of Port Lavaca, Texas, formed a powerful circle of influence during my early years. Family, friends, and teachers, as well as church and community leaders, filled my life in this place. Their wise instructions laid a deep foundation for my life. The members of my close-knit village often uttered words like *love, excellence, character, service,* and *honor.* More importantly, they modeled the meaning of these words for the children growing up in their midst.

Such words often came from my loving father and mother during these early years. They established firm rules which guided my behavior at home, at church, and in the community. Their consistent discipline was matched by a tangible and abiding love. They demonstrated their love for me not only by providing clothing, shelter, and necessities, but also by spending time with me. My parents both required and earned my respect. Though not perfect, they loved me consistently and practiced the behaviors they expected me to follow. They assured me I could achieve anything with hard work. Their wise and intentional parenting led me to make positive choices which have led to productive living.

As I look back on those early years, I understand now that our family would have been labeled "poor" by most people's standards. Yet, living in a happy home—one rich with love—contributed to my childhood notion that ours was a typical middle-class family. Indeed, my parents' principles for living have proven far more valuable than anything money could have purchased for me as a young child.

Outside of home, I found my church filled with wise and capable leaders. Biblical truths I learned at church were consistently reinforced at home. The Ten Commandments outlined the basic rules of living for me. My church also emphasized the value of obedience, generosity, and service. More than just rules for living, I learned the importance of a personal relationship with God. Even at an early age, I understood my responsibility to know God in a real way. No one ever hinted that I was too young to understand God or seek His guidance. Since the age of six, I have intentionally followed Jesus. My relationship with God did not happen only on Sundays or at church events. Time with God was also integrated into my home life, through prayer and weekly Bible study. My early years led to a lifetime of knowing and seeking God on a daily basis.

Along with family and church, my school experiences helped shape me in those early years. Throughout elementary school (1958-1964), the system of segregation meant that African American and Caucasian students did not attend the same schools. Negro teachers—also called "Colored"— taught Negro students in our schools. African Americans, as we are called today, learned from other African Americans in the school settings of my early years. Our instructors were honored leaders in the community where I lived. We respected them, heeding their wise words about life and learning.

In this segregated school setting, resourceful teachers often used creative methods to make learning simple, personalizing the lessons for each child. Our classrooms often lacked new books and educational tools, so teachers used common items to teach our lessons. For example, I learned fractions using popsicle sticks. My teacher sent us to the playground to find twenty popsicle sticks each. When we returned to our desks, she told us to place eight sticks on our desks. When we picked up two sticks, she said, "You are holding two-eighths." To this day, her lessons have made fractions easy for me to understand. A lack of resources in school never served as an excuse for a lack of learning.

Our teachers were present not just in school, but in local events and church activities, too. They regularly engaged parents in the educational process, working together to set goals for achievement. I will never forget one teacher informing my parents that my spelling skills needed to improve in order for me to succeed in college, particularly in college writing. This created a common expectation and a sense of accountability for me. Teachers and parents communicated often, and I truly sensed they all held similar hopes and dreams for me.

I left elementary school feeling safe and secure in my identity, and confident that I could do anything I desired. These early years gave me a solid foundation which led to success in other environments. Wisdom and direction from my childhood village remains a clear and guiding force in my life today.

LESSONS
LEARNED
from the Early Years

#1

ALWAYS DO YOUR BEST

Give 100% effort in everything you do. Do not make excuses or expect others to accept excuses.

In elementary school, my teachers let us know that they expected nothing less than our best effort at all times. They viewed these expectations as the foundation for accomplishing our goals and achieving great things. Our teachers constantly pushed us to find new levels of success. They never allowed us to feel satisfied until we had mastered a skill completely. One teacher posed a ridiculous question to prove this point. He asked, "If a doctor delivers one hundred babies and drops only 10 percent of them, is that satisfactory?"

Of course, his young students adamantly replied, "No!"

"Exactly!" responded our teacher. "The doctor has injured ten children because of his carelessness." While his example seemed extreme, his point stuck in our memories. Never accept *good* effort from yourself when *excellent* effort is required.

All of our teachers impressed upon us the importance of setting high standards for ourselves in every task. During my early years, I remember observing this principle often. On one occasion, a fellow classmate did not complete his homework. He explained to our teacher that the electricity in his home had been disconnected the previous night. His family did not have the money to pay their bill. Rather than accept this as an excuse, the teacher made him miss recess in order to do his work. She instructed him to make his school work a priority by doing his work while the sun was still shining. This way darkness would not force him to miss another assignment. At the time, her response seemed harsh, but it taught us all a valuable lesson. Some weeks later, we learned that this firm teacher was also a compassionate woman who quietly engaged others in the community to help the student's family pay their bill. To be sure, our community faced many kinds of hardships. However, people in my community did not use hardship as an excuse for failing to work hard.

#2
KNOW YOUR HISTORY

You are a reflection of all those who came before you. Represent them with right living and honor them with your accomplishments. Remember their sacrifices which have paved the way for your success.

As an African American child, I knew that my family and community expected me to do great things. My blood line includes queens and kings from Africa who built the pyramids. I embraced the fact that it is in my lineage to accomplish amazing feats. Moreover, teachers often spoke of talented African American leaders, scientists, mathematicians, and artists. Their teaching helped us to see ourselves in American history. These successful men and women looked like us— and they helped make America a celebrated country. Our teachers encouraged us to have what some call Black Pride. Simply put, this meant having pride in ourselves and our African American ancestors.

Learning the history of our people established a deep sense of dignity in us and birthed in us an unwavering confidence. As African

Americans, we understood our sacred responsibility to make our ancestors proud. After all, they sacrificed, and even died, for the opportunities we enjoyed. At a minimum, our teachers expected we should obtain a college degree, so that we would have good jobs and earn a stable living.

We felt the weight of those expectations. Our communities stressed that every action must reflect our pride in being African American. A teacher from my early years told a parable about a young man who was the only African American at a conference. He arrived late to meetings and failed to participate in group discussions. As the conference closed, several Caucasian leaders remarked that his actions proved how little African Americans contributed to society. My teacher concluded by saying, "While this stereotype is not true, you *must* act in ways that show the best of you as you represent our community."

His warning left a powerful impression. As young men and women of color, we accepted our duty to represent our people and their history. The treasure of knowing our history motivated us to pursue excellence in our daily lives.

#3
OBEY ADULTS

Obey parents, teacher, pastors, relatives, and friends. Their goal is to help you be the best person that you can be. It is their duty to help children grow and mature, learning standards for successful living.

To my parents, it was critical that children obey adults. My mother began training me to obey all instructions from adults before I turned two-years-old. As a toddler, I learned to obey the word "*no*" without questioning. My mother began by using this command to teach me never to move things in our home without permission. She knew that simple obedience like this would be the key to learning what adults wanted to teach me. Obedience brought discipline to my life and prepared me for the future.

Another standard my mother regularly taught was listening, and not speaking, when adults were speaking. This seemed quite a challenge for me as a child. But, consistent expectations about this behavior at home and at church helped shape good manners and respectful behavior over time. Once, someone at church reported that I had disobeyed in Sunday School. I told my parents that this was not true. However, my mother and father insisted that an adult would not deliberately lie about me. My parents believed the adult and expected me to change my behavior.

In my house, disobedience was a serious offense, and it led to serious consequences. Even slight disobedience led to punishments like restrictions from watching television or attending fun events. Sometimes, my parents required me to share my disobedience with another relative or adult who might further admonish or punish me. If I disobeyed in a serious way, my parents administered a physical spanking—or a "whipping"—that did not hurt me physically, but it hurt my pride more than anything else. Proverbs 13:24 states, "Whoever spares the rod hates their children, but the one who loves their children is careful to discipline them." While many today disagree, my parents believed that biblical instructions for parents included spanking as a part of discipline. Their consistent discipline taught me the value of obedience, which became a building block for my education.

#4

TRY NEW THINGS

As a child, learn to experiment and try new things, so that you learn your natural talents and skills, pleasures and dislikes, as well as strengths and weaknesses. This understanding is essential to discovering who you are. Be sure to consider your passions and strengths as you choose a career and decide on ways to serve your community.

Because I learned obedience at an early age, I instinctively trusted my mother's instructions. As a child, my mother required me to accept any new opportunities that came to me. She said I should try my best at something before dismissing it. That way, I might discover new passions and new talents I would not have known otherwise. My mother firmly believed in valuing new opportunities, and she often told community leaders how she felt. She said to them, "If you want Jennifer to do something, just tell her what you need her to do. She will do it."

She held this belief all the way through my youth. Her advice helped me realize many of my God-given gifts and abilities. It also helped me to become a respected member of the community. One day when I was in college, my mother's friend replied to her, "Since Jennifer is now eighteen and a young adult, I think that it is time for us to *ask* her if she will do certain things for the community."

My mother smiled and agreed. When I learned of this, I said to her, "You have taught me well. I can decide which things I must do, which things I am willing to do, and which things I am not willing to do." Because of my mother's strong leadership and wisdom in this area of life, I learned important things about myself. Her words paved the way for me to gain valuable skills, experiences, and confidence during my childhood years.

#5

TRUST GOD IN ALL THINGS

Trust God in all situations, believing that all things work together for the good of those that love the Lord. Life is composed of both victories and struggles. In God's hands, even our greatest difficulties can become productive times of learning.

During these early years, I was stricken with an illness which easily could have killed me or left me paralyzed. As a young child, I do not remember feeling afraid or worried at the time. Surely, though, my parents faced many fears, while the doctors waited to see if I would fully recover. The fervent, continual prayers of my parents and my church surrounded me during this time. One day, my pastor visited me. He reminded me to pray, to have faith in God, and to expect God to heal me. Even as a small child, I learned from the Bible that God healed many people from sickness and disease. My pastor let me know that God's Holy Spirit lives inside of every believer. This belief meant that God's power still heals people from sickness and disease.

With simple, childlike faith, I believed that God would do what He said. I placed my trust in God, never questioning whether He would heal me. And He did. God destroyed the illness in my body, allowing me to live a healthy life and a happy childhood. My family and community rejoiced in God's answer to our faithful prayers. Through this time, I learned to depend on God in the midst of trials.

Today, I embrace the truth of Romans 8:28: "We know that in all things God works for the good of those who love Him, who have been called according to His purpose" (*NIV*). But God does not always answer "*yes*" to everything I ask Him through prayer. Even so, He always deserves my trust. Sometimes, He answers "*wait*," and I reap rich rewards by waiting on His timing for my request. When God answers "*no*," He still teaches me valuable lessons when I am willing to trust Him. No matter the answer, I trust that God is for me in every situation I face.

ECHOES FROM THE EARLY YEARS

- **Respect your elders.** *They are important to your community, giving necessary counsel to the young. Respond to their needs.*
- **Strive to know and imitate great people**. *Find them, observe them, and seek to abide by the rules you observe them following.*
- **Be honest.** *Others will come to depend upon and respect you because of your honesty. Honesty is the foundation for strong character.*
- **Make your parents proud.** *Listen to lessons taught and live in ways that honor your parents, history, your people, and your God.*
- **Follow the Golden Rule (Matthew 7:12***). Think before you act. As you live with others, treat them the way you want to be treated.*
- **Love those who do evil to you (Romans 12:9).** *God alone has a right to seek revenge. Do not become a prisoner to unforgiveness.*
- **Give the tithe (Malachi 4:10***). Give 10 percent of your earnings to the church. Everything you have rightfully belongs to God.*
- **Study and work hard.** *Go early and stay late, working until you accomplish every goal in an outstanding manner.*
- **Dream big.** *Never let anyone say you cannot achieve something. Dream big dreams, and accomplish great things. You control your destiny.*

CHAPTER TWO

THE TEEN YEARS

Walking, I am listening to a deeper way. Suddenly, all my ancestors are behind me . . . You are the result of the love of thousands.

—*Linda Hogan*

Integration came to Port Lavaca when I began junior high school. As my classmates and I left our segregated elementary school, our teachers spoke key words of assurance over us. They demonstrated their pride in teaching us by boldly expressing their confidence in our ability to succeed. Reminding us that we had a debt to pay to many African Americans who sacrificed for our opportunities, they urged us to work hard and excel in school. The sense of pride these teachers imparted helped me accept the challenge before me. As I entered an integrated school system, the strong voices of these African American teachers would continue molding my life. All my elementary teachers had been African American, but all my middle school teachers would be Caucasian. While integration brought harsh realities, these things did not destroy me because of my parents' strong guidance, as well as encouragement from church and community leaders.

Based on stories in the newspaper, radio and television, I expected to encounter plenty of unjust situations in my new school. Indeed, my own experiences led me to fear such things. For example, Caucasian Americans sat at the counter to eat their ice cream at the local drug store, but African Americans were forced to stand. African American customers were never served before Caucasians, no matter how long they stood in line. Additionally, only Caucasian people could sit on the first floor of the movie theatre in our town, while African Americans were restricted to the balcony. Furthermore, when my parents hoped to build their home in a particular neighborhood, the city refused their request saying only Caucasian people could purchase land in that area. In those times, things like this happened frequently.

In my youth, these situations brought deep embarrassment. However, one particular encounter while on vacation in Mississippi frightened our whole family. A Negro man boarded the bus and had to stand even though empty seats remained at the front of the bus. At that time, unjust laws forced Negroes to sit at the back of the bus. Even so, one Caucasian man offered the Negro gentleman a seat at the front of the bus; however, another Caucasian man protested loudly. This situation made my father both angry and nervous. He clearly knew speaking up for the African American man could bring danger and harm to his family. In my youth, situations like this caused both resentment and humiliation.

Based on these kinds of shameful experiences, I anticipated race would impact school grades more than ability. To my surprise, I found skilled instructors and a fair grading system in my new school. Talented teachers who cared about all students engaged me in learning experiences that prepared me for the future. One Caucasian instructor in high school surprised me with her support. She visited my home to make sure my parents knew that I was a capable student. She wanted to make sure my parents had plans for me to go to college. Her efforts to earnestly share her thoughts with my parents shocked our family. Such interactions were uncommon in our community at the time, and they made a lasting impact on my life.

As I grew, teachers, parents, and community leaders continued to stress the value of hard work. They repeated words like "*excellence*", "*hard work*," "*respect*," and "*pride*." My parents made sure I completed homework assignments, and my teachers made sure classroom activities connected to real life. Key teachers forged strong relationships with my parents and me. Adults challenged me to strive for A's and B's on my report card. They insisted my future should include a college degree. One Latina teacher in high school stood out as exceptional because of her high expectations and fair treatment of all students. Though painful instances of unequal treatment still occurred, new relationships and experiences broadened my understanding of the world.

During my teen years, childhood friendships expanded to include new Caucasian friends. New opportunities in things like band and basketball meant chances for new friends; however, challenges remained. While school activities became integrated, church and community activities remained largely segregated. Sometimes my friends and I had difficulty finding our way through all the changes in our community. During this time, the Sunlight Girls Club provided a safe place for African American girls as they learned to navigate these transitions. One of my teachers from the segregated school developed this program to assist young African American girls. Here, we were in the racial majority, and we could discuss real problems and concerns with the African American women who mentored us. The Sunlight Girls Club helped us achieve academic success, equipped us with proper etiquette, matured us in character, and instilled in us critical leadership skills. As I steered through the waters of change in my newly integrated school environment, the Sunlight Girls Club made a significant difference for me. Through this club, I learned to become a young woman of distinction.

Parents worked alongside the Sunlight Girls Club to support our success. They raised funds for all of our activities. Through this fundraising, they taught us how to earn and manage money. The club provided rewards for good grades and excellent conduct in school. These rewards were often educational field trips in Texas and surrounding states. Our travels gave us experiences that our families might not have otherwise been able to provide for us. Also, mentors instructed us regarding how to dress, speak, and behave in ways that would bring us honor and opportunities. We learned to sit like ladies, crossing our legs at the ankles. We practiced speaking politely and using our words to lift up others. We gained the skills to hold club offices like president, treasurer, and parliamentarian. Participating in these group activities with strong adult leaders changed our young lives.

My teen years provide evidence that it truly takes a village to raise a child. At a recent reunion, many of us recalled the good things the Sunlight Girls Club built into our lives. We fondly remembered receiving a piece of luggage and a college scholarship from the club at graduation. Looking around the room, we saw teachers, nurses, businesswomen, military women, and even a college president. This is the legacy of Mrs. Naomi Chase, the Sunlight Girls Club founder. Undoubtedly, wise words from an entire community of people like Mrs. Chase helped launch a generation of successful women from Port Lavaca. While this stage of life could have been confusing and difficult, it was not such an unpleasant experience because of the loving efforts of many adults in my supportive village.

LESSONS
LEARNED
from the Teen Years

#6

MAKE TODAY COUNT

Your actions today will matter tomorrow. Do your best. You build your future one day at a time. A better tomorrow begins with actions you take today.

As a teen, I aimed towards the goal of a college education. Parents, teachers, and adults in my community came alongside me to help me achieve that goal. Because of their support, I had a clear vision for my future. They encouraged me to prepare myself and kept me focused on college. From them, I understood it would take many years of hard work to reach my goal. They wisely understood that the daily choices I made would impact my future success. They urged me to think often about my future. Keeping my future in view helped guide my actions each day in a positive way.

One teacher stressed the importance of making each day count in achieving our goals. She recounted a story to remind students how decisions we made today would determine what we accomplished tomorrow. The story involved a young man who saw an older gentleman sitting on a bench. The older man had only one arm. The young man felt deep compassion for the one-armed man. Instantly, the older man recognized the strong look of compassion on the young man's face. Noticing his concern, the older man began a conversation with the young man. He shared about his life, and he instructed the young man about his future. He explained that the choices the young man made today could impact his life forever. The man said, "I believe you have compassion for me because I have only one arm. I lost my arm when I was just about your age. I disobeyed my parents. They told me to stop jumping on my father's truck just as he was leaving for work, but I did not follow their instructions. Jumping on the truck, I fell and hurt my arm. The choice I made that day changed the rest of my life."

Choices have consequences. In order to reach a goal, one must make the right choices. Every day brings the opportunity to make new choices. When you are working toward a goal, make today count.

#7

NEVER RUN FROM A CHALLENGE

Even when life seems unfair, keep your eyes on the prize, working constantly to attain your goals.

I n high school, I noticed people were not always judged by their ability or character, but by the color of their skin. Striving for membership in the honor society, it surprised me that I was not accepted by my junior year. The grades and activities of Caucasian honor students appeared similar to mine. My parents inquired why I was not selected, and administrators replied that I lacked leadership involvement. I made plans to address this comment, so that I could accomplish my goal of joining the honor society.

My senior year, I sought out every possible leadership opportunity. Finally, the honor society invited me to join. I became only the second African American at my school to earn this distinction. I later learned that some of the organization's leaders had concerns about inviting me to join earlier. They feared problems if I traveled to conferences with them, since many hotels were closed to African Americans. Finding a place for me to stay would prove difficult, which was a concern for the school. They chose to resolve the problem by inviting me to join during my senior year, so I would graduate before the honor society traveled again.

In the midst of all this situation, my father continually stressed the importance of never quitting in the face of a challenge. He taught me to remain calm instead of getting angry, so that I could ask questions, get answers, and make sound decisions. He encouraged me to think and re-think situations before I took action. Additionally, my parents made sure I understood that hard work always reaps rewards. Even if I failed to reach a certain goal, they assured me the effort given would pay off in other ways. In this case, I eventually achieved my goal of joining the honor society. However, my academic efforts in pursuing that goal contributed to even greater achievements in my life.

#8

DEFINE EXCELLENCE

Set high standards for yourself. Develop a definition of excellence based on reading, observing great people, and submitting to rules. Then, strive for excellence as you participate in school, church, and community activities.

Excellence was a concept learned through the words and examples observed as a member of the Sunlight Girls Club. In 1960, Naomi Chase held deep concerns about young African American girls successfully transitioning into the newly integrated schools of Port Lavaca, TX. A "woman of action," she founded the Sunlight Girls Club that same year in her garage.[2] This organization helped girls ages 9-18 to define and pursue excellence. In the Sunlight Girls Club, excellence meant becoming a "lady of distinction." Girls learned rules for church, school, and community events. We learned to dress, sit, talk, and act like ladies. The Sunlight Girls Club also taught girls to type, sew, cook, and even how to dance at social occasions.

We learned principles of excellence in all aspects of life. Our club meetings included spotlight sessions on character development. Distinguished individuals spoke at our meetings. We also practiced excellence by using correct English and reciting poetry with expression.

Group celebrations included carefully chosen elements to represent our club colors of green and yellow. Written programs for ceremonies boasted beautiful artwork and were free from grammar and spelling errors. The Sunlight Girls Club imparted all these things and more. Today, when I think of Mrs. Naomi Chase, I often hear her voice and the wise words she shared with us. I remember that ladies always use decent language that raises someone up. I strive to never use foul curse words, or words that demean. I remember to sit like a lady, always crossing my legs at the ankles. I recall her emphasis on respect and service to others. Even today in difficult situations, I ask myself, "What would Mrs. Chase do in this setting?" Her example of excellence impacted an entire community and continues to reverberate today.

#9

ENGAGE IN GROWTH ACTIVITIES

Participate in activities that allow you to grow. Do not look to the right or to the left to see what others are doing. Take pride in participating in activities for growth, even if you go alone.

Attendance at church activities, bible study, and prayer groups continued throughout my teen years. But as I grew older, new activities in school made it more difficult to dedicate time to church opportunities. Still, my parents insisted that I work to stay engaged in these things that helped me grow spiritually. They made church activities a priority, because they knew they would bear good fruit in my life. My growth was important to them.

For me, one of the highlights of these years included participating in the Baptist Training Union program at church. Student participation was low; however, my parents made sure that I attended consistently. While I sometimes resented having to attend when other friends were engaging in fun activities on Sunday evenings, I learned discipline from my attendance, and I realized important spiritual truths in these

Bible studies. Baptist Training Union also presented me with opportunities other students were not given. Participating with my whole heart meant that I earned favor and recognition in the organization. For a number of years, adult leaders allowed me to be an officer for the program, prompting me to acquire important skills like public speaking. By remaining consistently engaged in this program, I came to understand that even if others choose not to, I must engage in activities that help me grow.

#10
DEVELOP DIVERSE FRIENDSHIPS

Develop relationships with people from all backgrounds. Look for friends whom you can trust, realizing they will come from various backgrounds. Seek to be a good friend to others, too.

Entering newly integrated schools, I feared that Caucasian students might not accept me. One critical incident helped me overcome this fear. As a member of the junior high basketball team, the coach asked each family to assist in driving team members to a nearby game. My family volunteered, but I was afraid that no one would ride with me, since I was African American. To my surprise, one girl said that she wanted to ride with my mother and me. Other Caucasian girls followed her lead and rode with us. The trip to and from the game provided a fun time for us to bond. With this simple act, we all began to discover the benefits of forming friendships with diverse people.

Later, I discovered that my teammate's mother had suggested she ride with my mother and me. This bold leadership act encouraged others to take a step in the same direction. For some of them, it was their first experience with an African American family. Considering the times, this gesture likely pushed my teammate outside of her comfort zone. Thankfully, she did not allow her discomfort to build a wall between us. Instead, she reached out to me. She led by her actions and helped me find acceptance.

I know I was not the only one who benefitted from this girl's leadership. Both African American and Caucasian American students faced changes in our newly integrated school. Change often brings fears and anxieties that can divide people. But entire communities benefit when people reach across issues that might divide them. Kindness and friendship lead to respect and cooperation. Looking back, I see now that my car ride to a junior high school basketball game was more than just a car ride. It was the beginning of my journey to embracing the value of diversity.

#11

GIVE LOVE AWAY

Love is not love until it is given away. Acts of love demand nothing in return.

Children learn the meaning of love from their families. Mine was truly a loving family. Growing up, we helped other family members who were sick or in trouble. We helped others when they needed assistance. My relatives and parents often expressed their belief that family members must support and care for one another. When my uncle was diagnosed with muscular dystrophy, he was unable to walk or use other parts of his body. My family regularly cooked for him and took food to his home. In later years, one of my aunts brought him to live with her. On many occasions, I witnessed my father go to her home to shave and bathe my uncle. This time demonstrated how my family cared for each other.

Loving others in the community was also part of my family's values. When someone needed financial assistance, our family donated to assist with the need. Our local church also embraced this same concept of love that gives. The church engaged us in activities like visiting the sick in hospitals. During these visits, we shared encouraging words and prayed for healing, comfort, and peace. We loved others through service.

Mother provided a strong example of this type of love. Visiting the elderly in nursing homes was one of her favorite activities. In December, she took the residents small gifts like socks and other necessities, which she purchased with her own money. Doing so always brought a smile to her face. She often said, "We give because we love." She embodied the lyrics from one of her favorite songs called "You Can't Beat God Giving," in which the lyrics state that we as people are unable to surpass the level of giving that God offers to us.[3]

ECHOES FROM THE TEEN YEARS

- **Go to college.** *Complete school, preparing to earn acceptance and scholarships for college. Education is the key to a decent life.*
- **Live peacefully together.** *People of diverse cultures, backgrounds, and religions must treat each other with respect.*
- **Plan for success.** *Clear goals, hard work, careful organization, and firm deadlines will help you accomplish your goals.*
- **Be a good friend.** *Be the kind of friend others can trust, realizing true friends can come from many different backgrounds.*
- **Respect yourself.** *Speak words and take actions which represent you well. Meet hatred and opposition with kindness and respect.*
- **Resolve conflicts.** *Admit when you are wrong. Share your point of view and listen to that of others. Never resort to fighting.*
- **Know and follow rules.** *Do this at school and in other organizations. If rules seem unfair, work peacefully for change.*
- **Do hard things.** *Never take the easy road that may lead to failure and destruction. Strong effort brings rich rewards.*
- **Attend church.** *Discipline and consistent attendance are important. Make this a priority, even if others do not.*

CHAPTER THREE

THE COLLEGE YEARS

The whole purpose of education is to turn mirrors into windows.

—Sydney J. Harris

Collegiate life at Hampton Institute, today known as Hampton University, equipped me with an essential education and led me to successfully complete two additional post-graduate degrees. In choosing a college, family members recommended Hampton because of its status as a historically Black university. They anticipated that Hampton would offer me the best chance to become all I could be in the next phase of life, since racial discrimination would occur infrequently there. Without the fear of discrimination, I did find Hampton a freeing experience. While this racial factor clearly influenced my college choice, I also selected Hampton due to its fine reputation, especially in the education department. Additionally, Hampton stood out because of its excellent professors and for its development of strong leaders like Booker T. Washington. During the Hampton years, my village of parents, church, and community leaders from Port Lavaca continued to provide sound advice. But I most recall guiding principles from remarkable professors, administrators, and student leaders whose lives reflected the wise words they spoke.

Engaging in classroom opportunities, along with observing authentic leaders in the faculty and student body, provided bedrock principles for life. Words and phrases like *"greatness," "world competition," "responsibility," "engagement,"* and *"Black Pride"* were engrained throughout Hampton's culture in ways that made a lasting impact. Here, exposure to new people and places created a dynamic force that changed my worldview. Leaving the small town of Port Lavaca, Texas, and moving to the Hampton community meant access to nearby large cities. Furthermore, these new places allowed educational encounters outside the classroom with great African Americans in many fields. Such beneficial experiences opened a world to me that made learning a joy and a pleasure.

The Hampton years developed both my academic life and my spiritual life. Worship and involvement in religious activities continued to prove important in college. Each week included Sunday church services, vesper mid-week services, and meetings with a Christian student group on campus. The college chaplain worked closely with many spiritual programs at Hampton. He modeled a life lived by godly principles, helping me to understand how important it is for Christians to "walk the talk," making sure their actions are consistent with biblical teachings. Moreover, students respected this man, because his behavior followed his beliefs. Because students respected him, his words carried authority—especially when he spoke at religious events. He was, indeed, a living example of the lessons learned from my earlier years in Port Lavaca.

Sunday worship services included sermons and speeches by ministers, rabbis, and spiritual leaders from numerous denominations. For the first time, I heard a Rabbi conduct worship. The music included beautifully delivered a cappella songs, along with gospel and some other unfamiliar styles. Learning about different ways to worship God was pleasant and stimulating. Moreover, these new worship experiences helped me gain knowledge about other religions and philosophies. These services cultivated a life-long openness to different expressions of worship and brought a certain depth and richness to my relationship with God that remains today.

Campus activities also included exposure to new and different traditions. One event in particular taught me the value of proper etiquette. I will never forget being invited on a Sunday to an activity at the president's home on campus. At Hampton, leaders stressed that a woman always dresses and behaves like a lady, and that clothes make a statement about the expected behaviors of the individual. For example, this unique occasion required young women to dress entirely in white. After I complained about this dress code, one dorm leader replied that sometimes in life, special occasions require special attire. She further explained the need to understand the customs and standards of others in situations like this event. Since she knew I would have future opportunities to travel abroad, she encouraged me to embrace this responsibility now. "When the time to travel comes," she stated, "Others will expect you to know proper ways to dress, sit, speak, and interact with people from other cultures."

Activities like this one in the president's home made campus life enjoyable and full, allowing me to build enriching relationships with different kinds of students. Attending Hampton Pirates athletic activities, such as basketball games, built a sense of community and group pride among students. Of course, on-campus and off-campus parties also provided fun and entertainment. As a sophomore at Hampton, joining the sisterhood of the Gamma Iota chapter of Delta Sigma Theta sorority was one of my most memorable activities. This fellowship and sisterhood with other women brought cherished memories. Participating in campus life alongside students, faculty, and administrators contributed to a vital spirit of community and Black Pride that lasted beyond my time at Hampton.

The total experience at Hampton Institute provided crucial lessons for my future. While Hampton did not provide formal mentorship from just one certain individual, it clearly fostered an environment full of fine examples for me to follow. I learned by observing great people, new ideas, and different cultures. Fresh opportunities and meaningful relationships made this a significant time in life. Hampton filled the college years with challenging classroom instruction, transformative religious activities, vibrant campus life, sorority sisterhood, unique travel opportunities, collaborative study groups, charitable service projects, and relevant community engagement. This undergraduate experience shaped *the whole person*. Even today, the Hampton experience remains a guiding force which informs many key decisions in my life.

LESSONS LEARNED

from the College Years

#12

PREPARE TO COMPETE

Learn all that you can, training to compete with the best in your field. Prepare to surpass those from your local area, state, nation, and world. At a minimum, this preparation requires acquiring another language, developing critical thinking and problem-solving skills, and learning to collaborate with people of diverse cultures and backgrounds.

A t Hampton, expectations for performance rose to a new level. I will never forget making a "C" on my first biology test as a college freshman. A number of other students found themselves in the same position. Our science instructor let us know that she knew we could do better. She declared that she would only accept our best efforts. Beyond that notion, she explained that the competition we faced came not only from other Hampton students, but from individuals at Harvard, Yale, Morehouse, and outstanding universities around the world. The words she spoke that day created a new desire to achieve exceptional learning every day, in every way.

Other instructors also embraced the idea of excellence shared in our freshman biology classroom that day. I discovered this theme consistently repeated by the faculty at Hampton, so much so that it became embedded in the university's core identity.

This brand of excellence, accompanied by a history program which taught about heroes and *she*-roes who looked just like me, instilled a deep sense of Black Pride during the college years. Additionally, classroom instructors promoted participation in study groups which included students with different ideologies and backgrounds. This kind of grouping was an important study technique that further prepared me to excel in future arenas of life that would be much broader and more diverse. Cooperative group learning proved both rewarding and enjoyable. This facet of learning strongly aided me in continuing to compete at a high level after college. My most notable successes have resulted directly from the principles of world-class excellence Hampton presented.

#13

CHANGE THE WORLD

Use your education to change the world. You must use your life to solve problems in your community. This commitment is especially true for people of color. If you fail to do this, who else will?

The 1974 graduation speaker at Hampton encouraged each graduate to know their history and to use it to help others. As African American college graduates, we were expected to tell the stories of our history. Traditional American history often omitted the outstanding contributions of important African Americans. As a result, many remained ignorant about our cultural achievements. Hampton had entrusted us with the stories of our history. Because we knew these stories, we needed to share them. Other people were not equipped to do so. Since we were fortunate enough to receive a college education, it became our responsibility to connect our people's past with our future. This forging of connections would ensure that the history of African Americans remained a part of both American and world history. In other words, the rich legacy of our people must be passed on by us.

The commencement speaker charged that every future generation must take up this same mantle of responsibility. He challenged us to commit to solving some problem that is "bigger than you." At Hampton, he said, we had some of the best minds in the country. He also pointed out that we had experiences which would compel us to become leaders. In these position, we could solve some of the world's greatest problems. He further noted that those in jail, on drugs, and who had few life goals could not do what was needed. It was up to us to improve the world for others. It was, in his words, the graduating call of 1974 to do the things in the world that needed doing and would long be remembered.

#14

EXPOSE YOURSELF TO GREATNESS

Seek to learn from those who achieve greatness. Do this in every area of life, learning from the finest leaders, teachers, scholars, and artists representing a variety of cultures.

Extra-curricular activities were an essential part of the Hampton experience. Through these activities, I met campus leaders, instructors, dorm assistants, and a variety of students. Such activities as the President's Tea and group discussions in professors' homes added a personal touch that made the campus feel accepting. As a history education major, my extra-curricular activities included visits to museums, participation in local political campaigns, and history club activities that brought classroom lessons to life. Additionally, Hampton students engaged with such renowned African Americans as poet Gwendolyn Brooks, Civil Rights leader Julian Bond, musicians Duke Ellington and Curtis Mayfield, as well as soul groups like the Stylistics and Ohio Players. All were great leaders in their respective

fields. Beginning in my college years, these kinds of interactions nur-
tured a lifelong thirst for greatness in me.

Furthermore, chances to travel to new places meant opportunities to
see great things. Visiting surrounding cities—whether through cultural
trips, sporting activities, college visits, or military base tours— enhanced
learning experiences for this small-town girl from South Texas. College
travels took me to Washington, D.C.; Philadelphia, Pennsylvania;
New Port News and Norfolk, Virginia; and Greensborough, North
Carolina. Beyond traveling off campus, Hampton classes included
students from all parts of the United States and many nations in
Africa. The world literally came to my doorstep at Hampton, and it
afforded me critical opportunities to explore vital topics from a wide
spectrum of viewpoints. Classmates with diverse backgrounds, whose
worldviews were quite different than mine, played a key role in my
education. Each of them pushed me to greater knowledge and deeper
understanding, making me a stronger member of society.

#15

SERVE OTHERS

It is your great honor and solemn duty to show love for others through service to mankind.

A vibrant Christian student organization held meetings in conjunction with our Hampton chapel services. The group included Christians from many different denominations, and it encouraged its members to work together in creating programs to serve others. Focusing on the needs of others united our group with a common goal. Our differences proved small in the light of our larger goal to serve members of the community.

This group initiated programs such as routinely visiting the nearby veteran's hospital. In this setting, we spent time with disabled and sick veterans who had bravely served our country. Some of the veterans had precious few family members or friends to visit them. Many were lonely and discouraged. As young college students, we stood in the gap and filled a deep need in their lives. Our visits provided the companionship and care they desperately needed and deserved. Through initiatives like this visiting of veterans, we witnessed firsthand the value of practicing servant leadership. It was a welcome opportunity for me to practice the value of service my parents taught me as a child in their home.

The Bible instructs Christians, "To whom much is given, from him much will be required" (Luke 12:48, *NKJV*). Our organization cited this truth and powerfully demonstrated it through meaningful acts of service like the ones in the veteran's hospital. From these expressions of love and service, I learned that servant leadership is the most valuable form of leadership. It transforms the lives of both the one who serves and the one who is served. This is the kind of leadership Hampton instilled in its students.

#16

SHARE YOUR FAITH

Be confident in God and seek both the faith and the skill to share your faith wherever you go.

During my upperclassman years in college, a particular experience as a Christian on campus affected me deeply. One evening after Bible study, I walked across campus with some friends to have refreshments at the student union building. As we walked, another group of friends greeted me along the way. With the realization that I still held a Bible in my hand, embarrassment overcame me. As I awkwardly shoved the Bible under my arm to avoid embarrassment, my friends stopped to talk with me. Later, as I reflected on my response that night, shame engulfed me. This moment caused me to look carefully at the evening's events.

Some introspection led me to request God's forgiveness for my behavior. The Bible clearly condemned my actions. Jesus said, ". . . Whoever disowns me before others, I will disown before my Father in heaven" (Matthew 10:33, *NIV*). In my heart, fear had kept me from acknowledging my faith in God to the friends I met on the way to the student union building. In hiding my Bible from them, I disowned the Lord before others.

In the days that followed, others discussed this incident with me. Their wise counsel and kind encouragement propelled me to make significant changes. Sharing my Christian faith with others became an essential part of my spiritual life. I overcame my embarrassment and discovered ways to share my faith within the Hampton community. I sought training that equipped me with the knowledge to confidently talk about my relationship with God. That one moment of shame served as a turning point in my spiritual life. Since that time, boldly sharing my faith has become a rewarding activity, which I seek to practice whenever the opportunity presents itself.

ECHOES FROM THE COLLEGE YEARS

- **Acquire deep learning.** *This requires reading, writing, and discussion. It can help solve the most challenging problems.*
- **Share your history with others.** *Use it to preserve and promote the greatness of your culture.*
- **Ask questions.** *This is the key to learning. It is a sign of strength to ask questions, seek answers, and pursue solutions.*
- **Make excellence your standard.** *A half-effort is never good enough. Maintain this standard in every part of your life.*
- **Learn about other cultures.** *Know the principles of the major world religions as you clearly define your own beliefs.*
- **Stay curious.** *Constantly seek to have experiences with different people from many cultures and places.*
- **Practice good citizenship.** *Involve yourself in the political process. Always vote in local, state, and national elections.*
- **Understand proper etiquette.** *Take time to learn the expected dress and behavior in various social situations.*
- **Have fun.** *Laugh often and create happy times, for they add value to life and bring joy to living.*

PART TWO

LEADERSHIP

CHAPTER FOUR

THE MENTORING YEARS

*No man is capable of self-improvement if he or she sees
no other models but himself.*

—*Conrado I. Generoso*

Securing my first job in Corpus Christi at the age of 22, I taught history for several years at a local junior high school. This area became home for about a decade, launching my career and resulting in many new adventures. Hampton Institute had well prepared me for the profession of my dreams. Equipped with a deep knowledge of Black history, integrating that knowledge into class curriculum brought joy and purpose to each day. After a few years, I obtained a master's degree in guidance counseling from Texas A & M University. This advanced degree led to a new job teaching high school history at the alternative education center, helping students who had fallen behind because of challenges like lengthy illnesses. Following this role, another local junior high campus extended an invitation to become their guidance counselor. Acquiring this new position brought special pride since the selection process included competition from several well-qualified candidates. All in all, these early professional experiences in Corpus Christi proved successful and enjoyable.

As a young teacher and emerging leader, one significant opportunity to share Black history with the broader community came when I was invited to help plan a year-long, city-wide bicentennial celebration in 1976. The city of Corpus Christi actively supported the event, which meant it would draw individuals from different cultures and many facets of life. In spite of my inexperience, a diverse leadership team welcomed my participation and eagerly embraced my enthusiasm for Black history. In fact, the efforts of our group ensured this important celebration of American history would include contributions from past and present African American leaders. Proudly, our work on the bicentennial celebration led to the establishment of Corpus Christi's Black History Cultural Committee, whose work continues today.

While employed as a teacher and counselor in Corpus Christi, leadership and character development played a prominent role in every experience. Professional, civic, and church leadership opportunities affirmed me, confirming that I held a great joy and a future path in leading people. Corpus Christi was a special time of personal growth, because it was filled with valuable mentoring experiences. Mature, dynamic leaders from various backgrounds spoke wise words that were long remembered. As I worked alongside these leaders, they often repeated words and phrases like *"mission," "vision," "communication,"* and *"conflict resolution."* Understanding such concepts chiseled me into an effective leader at a young age.

In addition to witnessing the practice of strong leadership principles, Christian leaders modeled a biblical foundation for living. Reminders to pray came often, allowing God to guide every decision.

They urged me to utilize my talents and skills in service to others. Moreover, they encouraged moral, ethical, and legal standards in every action. Strong servant leaders mentored me, imparting the defining values which guided them. They not only advised on difficult issues, but they also provided wise counsel on ways to strategically handle delicate situations. Over the years, such leaders became lifelong mentors whose relationships I cherished. Though several of these key leaders have passed away, they live on in my life as I deliberately act on the truths they shared. Memories of these mentors evoke an attitude of gratitude, due to their exceptional leadership and their great impact on my life. Such leaders embodied the biblical principle that the older men and women should guide and instruct the younger (Titus 2:3, *NIV*).

The mentors who shaped my young adult years came from many stations of life. For example, one pastor made a special contribution to these critical years in my journey. Nationally known for his work in evangelism and teaching, this man commanded the respect of people across all races and cultures. During the 1970s, he facilitated pulpit exchanges between Caucasian American churches and African American churches during Sunday night worship services. Furthermore, he exercised great foresight in affiliating his church with both the Southern Baptist Convention and the National Baptist Convention, which were divided along racial lines. Dual affiliation wisely gave his church access to the best of both Caucasian American and African American resources. At that time, bold leadership actions like his were unprecedented. This man's stellar example stands out among my experiences in Corpus Christi. Another significant mentor was an accomplished artist who could reach across aisles and bring people together. This Christian man cared deeply for others and used his talents to serve the community. When asked to run for city council, he smiled and turned down the request. Humbly declining the suggestion, he replied, "This would impact my creativity as an artist. There are other ways for me to serve. God is leading me in a different direction." Instead, he continued to design powerful and inspiring artwork, which was displayed throughout Texas. His influence, like his artwork, was a thing of enduring beauty.

Additionally, one other man served as an unlikely mentor. This elderly Christian gentleman, because of circumstances beyond his control, was never formally trained in reading and writing. However, the public knew him as a great community organizer, especially in fundraising events. With his relational giftedness, he masterfully designed teams of people and united them to accomplish a common goal. Among his great strengths were his understanding of people and his ability to resolve conflict peacefully. Strong women served as mentors, as well, always stressing the importance of meaningful relationships and the value of diversity. Often, today, I hear the voices of these exceptional leaders guiding me through tough decision-making periods.

The Corpus Christi years were ones that grounded me for future effective leadership and continuous Christian maturity and growth. Observing successful mentors led me to understand that individuals are respected when their actions are consistent with their words. Special leaders invested considerable time in me, and I knew that someday it would be time for me to do the same for others. Indeed, this stage of my development clearly illustrates the biblical principle from Luke 12:48: "From everyone who has been given much, much will be demanded; and from the one who has been entrusted with much, much more will be asked" (*NIV*).

LESSONS
LEARNED

from the Mentoring Years

#17

PLAN CAREFULLY

Initial team planning is important. Define, write, and discuss the mission, purpose, structure, and expectations of the team. A leader must value, respect, and understand the viewpoints of every group member, especially when members represents diverse cultures and organizations.

Once, in discussing an important task my team sought to complete, one leader shared with me the idea that work done in the beginning of a project can aid members in understanding the group's direction. This leader further noted that when individuals with different points of view come together, both written information and discussion assist with clarity. Additionally, those engaged in the work should have an opportunity to review written documents and provide feedback that could modify those documents. Though collaboration remains important, a leader must guide the process, so that conclusions are drawn and agreed upon in a timely manner. Remember, small groups are often ideally positioned for the task of initial planning. Work with a small group to communicate the initiative clearly, with a first draft of goals and objectives. Then, allow the larger group to react to the ideas of the smaller group.

Another mentor shared similar concepts when he offered the following advice: When planning a large event or a program with many concepts, do your homework. One effective approach includes clearly writing out goals and objectives for the project before sharing them. Research what others have done, so that you connect your work to the successful experiences of others. Once you have done this preparation, bring the concept to a group of three to five people. Be sure to solicit their feedback before explaining it to a larger group. Integrating this type of feedback often refines the goals and makes the presentation clearer when addressing larger groups. Engaging others in this process also allows them to develop a sense of ownership in the goals and objectives the team seeks to accomplish. Remember that strong leaders always begin with the end in mind.

#18

COMMUNICATE YOUR VISION

When establishing a vision, communicate the vision so that individuals from diverse backgrounds grasp it firmly. The vision must be presented so that they see, hear, smell, and experience it in such ways that they are able to implement it.

A mentor said once when I was tired of working on a project that I needed to be patient and spend more time communicating and discussing my vision. He further stated that in a large organization, each individual relates to the vision differently. Their perspective is directly affected by their distinctive role in the organization. The vision becomes unique to each person in the group, as the leader connects it to the work each person does for the organization. With this in mind, leaders must think of ways to communicate the vision in a way that it becomes personal to every individual group member. Brainstorming sessions and small group discussion can help achieve this desired effect. When everyone is on board, the group's energy and efforts all become focused in the same direction.

At every stage of the group's work, the leader must remember that the vision will be obvious to him or her well before others fully embrace it. Leaders must accept this as a fact of leadership, thereby working to effectively share their vision with group members who must help them execute it. To achieve this goal, accomplished leaders strive to communicate in ways that help others see the plan in the same way as the leader and make meaning of their part in the process. The patience and creativity required to do this work is often the hardest part of leading any group. Utilizing different mediums of communication that stimulate the five different senses can prove to be a successful approach in leading teams to embrace a unified vision and achieve goals.

The Bible also recognizes the importance of these concepts, as it states in Proverbs 29:18 that without "vision, the people perish" (*KJV*). Wise leaders, like my mentors, possess a deep understanding of the important role intentional communication can play in establishing vision.

#19

RESOLVE CONFLICT

Whenever a conflict is anticipated, wise leaders will conduct a "meeting before the meeting" with key group members in order to resolve potential issues that could derail a planned meeting of the entire group.

A t a particular meeting I facilitated, one issue took up nearly all of the meeting time, because it related to a matter that caused great conflict within the group. Tensions between a few group members resulted in an explosion of emotion and passion on each side. Sadly, heated conversation led to an exchange of words some members later regretted. After the meeting, one of my mentors asked me if I knew that this agenda item was a source of such great conflict. I replied that I did, indeed, know about these tensions. With deep surprise, he stopped and admonished me by saying, "Let me suggest that you should have pulled the various parties together to see if they could reach a compromise before the meeting." He further explained that he often called this strategy the "meeting before the meeting."

Confronting conflicts in a constructive manner can result in positive outcomes; however, good facilitation must occur within a framework of clearly established rules for discussion. These kinds of boundaries are a necessary safeguard when viewpoints begin to clash. In a conflict, each point of view needs to be heard, and firm guidelines for civil discussion help accomplish this goal. Opposing sides of an issue need to listen carefully to one another, without making accusations or defending themselves. Leaders must create a safe environment for each side to state their concerns before a peaceful resolution can occur.

Sometimes, we learn by proactively following sound advice. Other times, we learn from disastrous mistakes we make. In this case, I learned from both. In future leadership roles, this mentor's wise counsel kept me from repeating a painful mistake.

#20
DO NOT SEEK VENGEANCE

When someone assaults your character, acts of retaliation never represent the wisest course of action. A good reputation, produced by moral and ethical living, can effectively combat untrue accusations.

A troubling situation occurred when a certain person in the community spread serious lies about me. Even worse, many believed these false rumors. This incited an attitude of retaliation in me. After some time, I had the opportunity to discuss this issue with one of my pastors. He listened to my angry ravings, and then he shared some sage advice. I will never forget his counsel on that occasion: *Live a good life and never chase a lie, for a good life will outlive a lie every time.*

At the time, his words were difficult for me to understand. He patiently explained that a lifestyle of consistent honesty, valor, and respect—rather than words, whispers, and rumors—define a person's character. Moral and ethical living form a sturdy defense when someone seeks to assault your character. People who hear false accusations about you will measure those accusations against their personal experience with you. They will also share their true experiences with others. In this way, you need not defend yourself, because others will do it for you. He instructed me to simply let how I lived handle the situation. While not at all sure of his advice, I accepted his guidance and acted accordingly. To my surprise, the situation was resolved in a manner similar to what he described. Today, I regularly counsel others that good living can often destroy false truths. My pastor further instructed me that in the face of mistreatment, I must always respond in love. He believed that life frequently finds a way of bringing about justice, and he suggested that many times a false accuser later finds himself needing to apologize for his lies. In light of this suggestion, he insisted that everyone must love even their enemies, as peace often comes from truly forgiving those who have hurt us. Anger, he warned, can eat at your soul, causing misery and sickness. He wisely supported his words with scripture, drawing from Romans 12:17 -19: "Repay no one evil for evil . . . do not avenge yourselves . . . for it is written, 'Vengeance is Mine, I will repay,' says the Lord" (*NKJV*).

ECHOES FROM THE
MENTORING YEARS

- **Research solutions.** *Do not reinvent the wheel to solve problems. Build programs and initiatives on the experiences of others.*

- **Establish an agenda.** *Do this for all meetings, setting clear objectives and timelines.*

- **Keep track of time.** *Have someone in charge of keeping the time, so that the meetings are finished as scheduled.*

- **Appoint a facilitator.** *In meetings, this person moves the group through the agenda efficiently and successfully.*

- **Form relationships.** *To lead communities, you must earn respect by becoming involved in activities with those you want to serve.*

- **Connect to local programs.** *Also join with state and national programs to maximize your impact on shared concerns.*

- **Practice Christian disciplines.** *Include consistent prayer and Bible study as you seek to live according to God's will daily.*

- **Take action.** *Engage in work that uses your talents, gifts, and skills to build God's Kingdom . . . inside and outside of the church.*

- **Give back**. *When someone invests in you, take seriously the responsibility of returning that investment by helping others.*
- **Do the work God calls you to do**. *Study and pray, then rise and work. In this way, your praying is connected to the work you do.*

CHAPTER FIVE

THE VERNON AND CEDAR VALLEY YEARS

Coming together is the beginning. Keeping together is progress. Working together is success.

—*Henry Ford*

After seven years as a teacher and counselor in Corpus Christi, I met my husband. Later, in August 1979, we got married. He has provided steadfast leadership for our family and critical support for my career through the years. His duties in the Air Force moved us to Wichita Falls, Texas. Something unexpected occurred as I searched for a job in this community. After months of prayer and seeking, I left the public school setting to accept a position at a community college. Through this move, I embarked on a new career path. This new start began thirty years of serving the public, through the work of four community colleges in two different states.

During these years, my work as a faculty member and administrator led me to realize that I truly wanted to advance my career within a community college setting. These years also allowed me to gain additional leadership skills, as I continued to observe powerful leaders across various college organizations. Such leaders enriched their communities, as they accomplished strategic goals and objectives by bringing people together around a common mission and vision. Witnessing effective leadership at every level, I benefitted from mature leaders who took time to impart their leadership philosophies and styles.

My first community college position was at Vernon Regional Community College, today known as Vernon College, on the satellite campus of Sheppard Air Force Base. In this capacity, I interacted with leaders on both campuses and in the military educational office. As an administrative counselor, the wide-ranging scope of this position incorporated a variety of responsibilities. Work in student services included overseeing registration, designing orientation, managing transcripts, and responding to student complaints. Another facet of the job meant advising and counseling students. Additionally, I served as campus representative for Sheppard's satellite campus in meetings at the main campus. Reporting directly to two supervisors created an ideal opportunity to gain a comprehensive understanding of the structure and organization within community colleges. From these supervisors and a team of experienced faculty, I began to grasp the knowledge and practices needed to effectively lead in an educational setting.

The Vernon experience enriched my career by teaching me about teamwork. As a new professional at Vernon, a team of strong and mature leaders invested in me. Their investment allowed opportunities to learn from those ahead of me on the journey. I shared one goal with these men and women—a strong desire to contribute to student success. A mature and effective team, they debated complex issues and resolved conflict in a productive way. This team developed valuable programs that enhanced achievement for all students. I learned the foundational practices of strong teamwork from this cohesive group. Their rare unity of purpose inspired me to embrace the importance of strong teams and solid relationships. To create an effective learning environment, these things are non-negotiable. Observing the collaboration of this dynamic team challenged me to grow professionally and increased my knowledge of the community college.

Work and family competed for my attention, as I learned to balance the demands of marriage and a new career. My Christian growth continued, with special emphasis on becoming a godly wife to my new husband. In Wichita Falls, our family united with two different congregations. Following the pattern of living I learned in Corpus Christi, I engaged in various community activities connected to both my church and my job. Serving in these arenas taught me the importance of learning to hear God's voice through prayer. Soon, prayer would guide another critical decision in the life of our family.

In 1984, my husband left the military. Our move to the Dallas Metroplex area saw the birth of our beloved son. A short period of time as a stay-at-home mom followed his arrival. However, through much prayer and discussion, my husband and I agreed on my return to the professional world. Securing an instructional associate (IA) position at Cedar Valley College, this campus of the Dallas County Community College District (DCCCD) presented exciting opportunities to advance my career.

As an IA and the Director of Women's Programs at Cedar Valley, major responsibilities included coordinating activities for returning adult women students. The job offered the chance to shape programs delivered by the Counseling and Advising Center. To successfully design such programs, I drew on my Vernon experiences and philosophies of student success learned there. Sharing this passion for student success, my supervisor integrated many of my ideas into the center's work. In these efforts, reporting to others in authority made it necessary to communicate openly and effectively. This strong communication encouraged their guidance, input, and approval for my ideas. Learning these communication skills helped me thrive both at Cedar Valley and in future positions.

During these professional years, strong supervisors, exceptional faculty, and outstanding counselors willingly invested their time in me. As a novice in a new field of work, meaningful conversations with such leaders brought maturity and growth. They shared ideas, concepts, and thoughts that later became words of wisdom embedded deep in the fabric of my life. Words like *"relationships," "strong teams," "effective communication,"* and *"student success"* echoed throughout our discussions during these years. It took time for me to fully grasp many truths they shared, but the mark these leaders made on me was undeniable. Experiences and observations from time with these supervisors, faculty, and counselors provided much of the advice I share with others today. Moreover, God continued guiding my steps as new experiences added spiritual growth opportunities to professional ones.

LESSONS LEARNED

*from the Vernon and
Cedar Valley Years*

#21

BUILD STRONG TEAMS

Develop cross-functional teams by ensuring that teams include members from all areas of the organization. Also, engage teams in activities designed to build strong relationships. This is critical to forming effective teams of people who cooperate successfully.

A significant part of the culture at Vernon included collaborative team work. For example, a faculty group worked across disciplines, making sure students achieved desired learning outcomes. As a newcomer from a different department in the college, faculty eagerly welcomed me into their work and taught me the importance of serving the whole student—including their emotional needs, home life, and other personal factors. Although I was a student services professional, this faculty group partnered with me, making certain that instructors and student services worked as one unit—not two separate units—to focus on student success. Team members not only focused on outcomes for their individual disciplines, but also discussed strengths and weaknesses of the whole college curriculum.

Integrating core instruction into all programs helped us to discover and improve weaknesses in our curriculum. For example, our team emphasized reading and writing skills by embedding them into all courses and programs. To make these changes, our team utilized reliable data about student achievement levels. Indeed, a strong culture of teamwork enabled us to achieve such goals.

In addition to focusing on clear objectives, team leaders fostered strong personal relationships on the team. They intentionally organized social opportunities, special gatherings, and holiday celebrations. Spending time together in these more relaxed venues allowed us to get to know and understand one another. Conversations as we traveled to meetings together also helped develop meaningful friendships among team members. Moreover, we learned to value the diversity on our team. While our team included some racial diversity, we were most diverse in terms of our opinions on various issues. Our clear respect for one another permitted rich discussion about many important matters. This attitude shaped our view of the students we served, too. At the Sheppard Air Force Base extension of Vernon Regional, our military students came from a wide variety of ethnicities, races, cultures, languages, and backgrounds. Learning to value each member of our team led us to value students as individuals. With this mindset, it seemed natural for us to focus on ensuring that each student, no matter his or her background, achieved success on our campus. My years at Vernon plainly showed that strong teams make for strong institutions.

#22

COMMUNICATE CLEARLY

Frequent and direct communication results in clear expectations and aids in organizational success, including vertical communication with supervisors, as well as lateral communication with co-workers.

At Vernon Regional Community College, working on two different campuses meant reporting to two different supervisors. This situation taught me the importance of understanding the distinct leadership styles of those in authority. It also taught me the importance of communicating to leaders in ways that align with their individual approach to the job. The two supervisors at Vernon, both dynamic leaders, approached leadership in quite opposite ways, requiring me to clearly understand the approach each preferred. Each supervisor took the time to share their beliefs and convictions about leadership with me. Paying attention to this nuance aided me in making sure that my communications were well-received and clearly understood. In accomplishing this, I became a trusted ally to each supervisor, as we worked together for the good of the students and the entire organization.

Good two-way communication with both supervisors and team members was critical to establishing clear expectations about our initiatives for student success. Good communication meant keeping supervisors informed about problems, triumphs, and opportunities. Supervisors communicated with me often to discuss our dreams and plans for students. At that time, we used written memos and telephone calls as the primary methods of communication. Today, new mediums of communication like email, text messages, and video chatting serve a similar purpose. During these early professional years, in a position with new administrative responsibilities, I observed and learned the vital role of clear communication when seeking to maintain trusting relationships.

#23

CLEARLY DEFINE EXPECTATIONS

Clearly define the roles and expectations for all those working in an organization. Spell out the specific responsibilities for each member on the team. Provide explicit expectations for behavior and performance.

Working extensively with members of the Air Force at Vernon Regional, I witnessed the military lifestyle on a daily basis. Interactions with military members of our team allowed me to observe the positive impact of clearly defined rules and regulations. Specific codes of behavior governed military interactions in ways that were unfamiliar to me. For example, I learned to respectfully stand whenever the general entered a room, and one never turned his or her back on the general. Similarly, the details of military dress code also made a distinct impression on me. Uniform specifications were precise, and the Air Force held its members accountable to the exact uniform guidelines. While such practices seemed foreign to me, I noticed the spirit of discipline they promoted.

While I was not always excited about the many rules and detailed policies which guide military life, I learned the intrinsic value of these kind of guidelines. The strict structure and organization of the military created a working environment with clear expectations. People were not confused about their roles and responsibilities, since these were always clearly articulated. As a result, team members completed their assignments efficiently. Meeting goals and objectives happened more easily when each person knew their assigned tasks. This organizational principle offered clear guidance for my future work in community colleges.

#24

SEEK AND ACCEPT FEEDBACK

Actively seek and accept feedback from people in different levels of your organization, as well as from those you serve. Strive to integrate their suggestions into your initiatives whenever possible.

In designing programs for women and other students at Cedar Valley College, I learned the importance of first seeking feedback from individuals in various sectors of the college. Since faculty members worked at the core level of our organization, it seemed especially important to engage them in creating new programs and establishing desired outcomes. Additionally, since students were the target audience for our programs, it seemed equally important to learn what they needed, desired, and expected. This approach gained strong support from supervisors and counselors alike, because they understood the importance of engaging faculty and students in developing successful initiatives.

For example, I represented the Counseling and Advising Center by designing a career fair that incorporated input from the voices of both students and faculty. In doing so, the Counseling and Advising Center acted on student requests to connect them directly with professionals who could share different career paths related to specific degrees plans. Making these connections helped students discover a variety of jobs they could obtain by utilizing their individual degrees. The students' feedback helped our event become more relevant, because it met a practical need.

Another suggestion from faculty in the music department resulted in a demonstration of electronic keyboards at this event. Because keyboards were a new technology at the time, this demonstration exposed our music students to several new career opportunities related to this technology. The faculty's guidance directly assisted students by presenting cutting edge career possibilities in the music field. As different units collaborated for the good of all students, I realized the wisdom and benefit of seeking and accepting feedback from others. This practice multiplied the impact of our efforts at the career fair and raised the bar for our entire organization.

#25

LISTEN FOR GOD'S VOICE

God can speak clearly and precisely to our hearts, if we listen intentionally for His voice. He can use the words of others, and even song lyrics, to speak directly into situations in our own lives.

I n Wichita Falls, I experienced a life-changing encounter with God. Prayer already occupied an important place in my life, especially in seeking guidance and wisdom. Knowing God spoke through the Bible, prayer, and the counsel of others, I relied heavily on these things. Even so, I felt inexperienced in hearing and recognizing God's voice directly in my life. On one occasion in Wichita Falls, that all changed. For the first time, I heard God's voice as clearly as if we were face-to-face.

The way in which God spoke remains as clear to me today as it was thirty years ago. One Sunday after church, someone asked if I would become the new pianist for the children's choir. Even having previous experience as a music minister and youth choir pianist, I had little confidence in my ability to do this job. Never having learned to play by ear like most musicians, music was not my greatest talent. Playing piano for the children's choir would require some skills that I lacked. Doubt crept into my mind, and I resolved not to make a decision about this matter without significant prayer. In truth, I assumed this was not something God wanted me to do at the time.

One day while listening to the radio, I heard a moving song. The sound was James Cleveland's arrangement of "God Uses Ordinary People" played over the airwaves. In that moment, it seemed as if the words of the song spoke directly to me. The singer crooned lyrics that told of how, when something is placed in "the Master's hands," He can make something out of nothing and turn a little into a lot. I knew immediately that this was God's voice telling me to play for the children's choir. At first, I argued with God in my mind, recounting all my musical insufficiencies. Continuing to listen, God's voice became undeniably clear. Indeed, God was speaking. He promised to provide everything needed for the task ahead, so I accepted the position. Serving as the children's choir pianist showed me that, indeed, God uses us in unique ways at different times in our lives. Our responsibility remains always to yield our hearts and wills to Him at every turn. Moving forward in my personal and professional life, listening to God became real in tangible new ways.

ECHOES FROM THE VERNON AND CEDAR VALLEY YEARS

- **Engage those at the core of your organization.** *Reach out to those working at the ground level of your efforts. In educational arenas, this means reaching out to faculty members who lie at the core of the teaching process, as well as staff and administrators.*

- **Value representation from all members.** *Invite individuals representing all areas of an organization to work together on the goals and objectives of the institution.*

- **Seek unity of purpose.** *Each entity and person must understand their contribution and connect their actions to a common goal.*

- **Provide adequate feedback.** *Develop clear expectations for teams, providing regular reports which detail information on progress. Use data to evaluate the success of team efforts.*

- **Identify effective communication strategies.** *Consider scheduled systematic reports, both written and verbal.*

- **Define your leadership style and philosophy.** *Also recognize those of your supervisors and team members. Such understanding aids in effective communication and leads to organizational success.*

- **Write down the rules and codes of behavior**. *Make written policies, rules, and standards available to everyone on the team. Specifically describe acceptable behaviors and manners.*

- **Encourage emerging leaders.** *Create an environment where everyone is comfortable expressing their dreams for the organization. Recognize leadership at all levels, and give approval for leaders to act on their dreams whenever possible.*

CHAPTER SIX

THE BROOKHAVEN YEARS

A mentor is someone who allows you to see the higher part of yourself,
when sometimes it becomes hidden to your own view.

—Oprah Winfrey

ontinuing my work with the Dallas County Community College District (DCCCD), I accepted a new position on the campus of Brookhaven College. There, I served in a series of positions beginning as a faculty counselor, moving to the Director of Counseling, and advancing to the Dean of Student Support Services and Human Development Services. This college was an exciting place to work and learn from vibrant presidents, administrators, and faculty. Expertise gained here as a faculty counselor propelled me into higher level administrative experiences and informed my approach as an administrator. I knew at a deep level the importance of involving faculty in my future administrative efforts. The decade spent at Brookhaven enriched my philosophy of leadership and convinced me that leaders must truly model the way for their organization. Moreover,

I embraced the truth that leaders must live authentic lives according to their personal values.

While having thoroughly enjoyed the work at Cedar Valley College, the Brookhaven position represented a career advancement. It was at Brookhaven I committed to a lifetime career in the community college setting, because it resonated closely with my personal value system. Community colleges play a unique role in serving the public. Their mission focuses on providing a quality education for students, often those seeking a second chance at a college education. They provide a variety of pathways to employment and enrichment for adult learners. Additionally, they provide dual enrollment opportunities for high school students to carry credits earned from high school into college. Moreover, community colleges dedicate themselves to bringing much needed resources to their local communities. Indeed, after more than thirty years of working, my commitment to the work of the community colleges remains among the greatest joys of my life.

The Brookhaven experience became a solid foundation for future career opportunities, because it was a rich, fertile environment conducive to personal and professional growth. I have often said, "I grew up at Brookhaven." These years matured me—making me a stronger person and clarifying my beliefs about the education of adult learners. Working alongside outstanding leaders exposed me to effective, new practices that guided me to participate in innovative, rewarding projects. Such experiences confirmed my desire to move from faculty to an administrative position on campus. This career shift meant that I began to study leadership with new intensity. I quickly realized that skills obtained as a teacher and counselor would prove crucial to the work of any administrator. For example, administrators and counselors alike must work with others, develop leaderships teams, and facilitate common goals. Likewise, administrators must often engage in the teaching process, as they share concepts and unite others in order to work toward a common vision. It seemed clear that God had ordered my steps to prepare me with the skills needed to succeed in becoming an administrator. Seeing God's clear hand in this preparation confirmed to me that this path, indeed, was His will.

During these years, the college presidents with whom I worked at Brookhaven showed tremendous commitment to students. One particular president took her time to mentor me. In fact, she was the first person to suggest that I should consider becoming a community college president. At the time, this thought was far from my mind, but I did continue to learn more about leadership and seek new administrative positions. Many hours of conversation with this president allowed me to share my best thinking about leadership and learn her thoughts about effective ways to lead others. Additionally, observing her leadership style led to my own understanding of several powerful concepts and principles, which I integrated into my own personal style of leadership.

Furthermore, the counselors on Brookhaven's campus represented some of the nation's best. Campuses around the country often adopted the programs developed by Brookhaven's counselors. Such programs included one that aided young adults in transitioning from living at home to living on their own. Another often emulated program assisted returning adult women, by connecting them with successful female peers in a mentoring situation. One of these exceptional counselors greatly impacted me by affirming a part of my learning style that I had yet to identify. Once, in sharing with her my gratitude for the people at Brookhaven who taught me so much, she replied, "Jennifer, people invest in you by sharing their experiences, because you seek to learn from others." While this fact was not evident to me then, I reflected on it and made it a deliberate approach to all future learning. Now, I can plainly see that seeking to discuss important issues with mature individuals from diverse backgrounds furthered my knowledge and skills in critical ways. In fact, this favorite learning strategy contributed to nearly all my future successes.

Alongside the significant professional growth of my Brookhaven years, I continued to grow spiritually. I enjoyed worship services, Sunday school, and Bible study, along with ministering in the children's department at church. Forming strong relationships with mature Christians, I pursued the biblical principle found in Titus 2:3-4 (*ESV*): "Older women . . . are to teach what is good, and so train the young women." Doing this prepared me, in time, to become one of the older, wiser women who could mentor young women in the future. While I still considered myself a young woman, I knew someday that I would be the older woman. Learning from seasoned Christian men and women equipped and prepared me for the upcoming role I would play in years to come.

Overall, the Brookhaven College years provided an essential period of growth. Meaningful discussions with respected leaders became a way of living and learning. I embraced the responsibility of listening to understand others, which in turn helped others to receive what I wanted to say. Paying close attention, I often heard phrases like "*open and honest communication,*" "*effective teams,*" "*value diversity,*" "*vary your communication,*" and "*listen to God.*" These ideas resounded in new and complex ways. Moreover, I began to realize how God's evident guidance in previous positions had equipped me with strategic knowledge and skills. Truly, God continued to ensure "that all things work[ed] together for [my] good" and His glory (Romans 8:28, *NKJV*).

LESSONS
LEARNED

from the Brookhaven Years

#26

AVOID FILTERED COMMUNICATION

Do not be guilty of filtering communication. In discussing important subjects, avoid communicating with only those in executive leadership. Intentionally seek to communicate with representatives from different areas of your organization.

The leader at the helm of any organization runs the risk of listening only to those in his or her inner circle. If this happens, the head of the organization will not accurately perceive the organization as a whole. Instead, he or she will receive feedback from only one perspective—that of executive leadership. In other words, when the leader seeks necessary feedback, it will be filtered through the eyes of the executive team. This limited view may result in the leader receiving incomplete or inaccurate information on any given issue. One must work to avoid this leadership pitfall at all costs.

At Brookhaven, the campus president engaged people throughout the campus in many different activities. In this way, she developed a common bond with team members, in order to learn their perspective of the organization. In an effort to unite people behind a common cause, she once invited individuals from every department in the college to enjoy a home cooked meal at her house. The intimate atmosphere encouraged casual conversation, as well as discussions about the goals of the college. Over the course of the evening, team members became better acquainted with the president and gained new insights about her vision for the college.

In another effort to promote communication, she invited team members to join in reading a strategic book related to her goals for the college. For example, in studying Richard Rodriguez's *Hunger of Memory*,[4] the president heard from those across the organization on how the concepts in the book could be used to promote valuing diversity in all areas of the college. This book explores the impact a single dominant culture has on minority members of an organization. As a group, we came to realize the negative impact of failing to integrate minority values and experiences into the fiber of our college. This led us to take intentional steps toward establishing Brookhaven as an international campus.

Additionally, this same president insisted that leaders must schedule open office hours. She regularly reserved a weekly block of time for anyone in the college to come speak to her without an appointment. Some individuals felt passionately about different issues, and these blocks of time ensured the president kept her finger on the pulse of issues that mattered to individuals at Brookhaven. Such meetings strengthened her relationships throughout the campus and created opportunities to address subjects that were not already on her radar. Furthermore, the president often walked the campus to increase her visibility and accessibility to students, faculty, and staff. In choosing to regularly leave her office, she avoided working in isolation. These practices enhanced her level of personal influence, because she wisely sought to communicate with team members throughout the organization.

#27

VALUE DIVERSITY

Value individual people and the diversity they bring to your organization. Diversity, international competency, and equity programs must be part of professional development activities for your team. Include field trips and study abroad opportunities.

Effective leaders must foster a climate of acceptance for diverse groups to become a part of the organization's culture. For example, I remember once suggesting Brookhaven's president should visit a historically Black institution. I wanted her to fully comprehend what existed there for African American students that was not available to this population on our own campus. To my surprise, she acted on my advice. She traveled to Atlanta with me and one other team member who had graduated from a historically Black university. We stayed several days, visiting universities such as Morehouse, Spellman, Clark Atlanta, and Morris Brown. Throughout our trip, we observed the unique touches that convey African American history and identity to students on these campuses. In Atlanta, this fine president grasped what it means for people of color to feel celebrated.

At the end of our time with students, administrators, and faculty from several different institutions, she replied simply, "I see and feel it everywhere. Now I understand what students get here that we must get busy developing at Brookhaven." In response, she developed a team of African Americans who worked together to develop programs that spoke to the needs of African American students. Because there was not campus-wide support for such programs, the president's whole-hearted support proved essential to the success of these initiatives.

Every organization must develop deliberate strategies for valuing diversity. They must clearly define the desired outcomes of these efforts. Executive leaders must commit to professional development activities which promote the value of diversity among all employee groups. Additionally, such leaders must seek to measure the tangible success of such activities. Creating an environment where diverse individuals can learn from one another must take significant priority in order to achieve these goals. The results, however, are worth the investment.

#28

KNOW YOUR VALUES

Know your authentic, true, genuine self, and clearly define your core values. Seek to live in ways consistent with your values, no matter the costs.

Strong personal values must guide your approach to leadership. Take time to articulate your core values. Write them down, asking individuals in the organization to hold you accountable for your actions and attitudes. While this accountability might be painful at times, it will provide an accurate reflection of your successes and struggles. You must understand who you are at your very essence before you can ensure you are living a consistent, authentic life.

Authentic leaders possess a deep commitment to honesty, a strong work ethic, and a willingness to act in ways they want others to emulate. To achieve these ideals, visibly display your core values in a place where you can see them often throughout the day. Even better, display them in a spot where others can see them, too. I distinctly recall observing Brookhaven's president do this very thing. She wrote down her values and shared them with the entire campus in a written form. I kept her values prominently posted on my bulletin board. Furthermore, I requested a meeting to discuss them with her. She shared more about what she had written and the experiences that led her to articulate these values. Our conversation increased the respect and level of trust between us. She said that day, "When you see me not acting consistent with these values, call me on it. We must all work together to model who we say that we are." Her sheer vulnerability led in the direction she wanted others to follow. Her transparency multiplied her influence within the organization. And her authenticity set a standard for all those around her. As the campus leader, she truly modeled the way for us all.

#29

COMMUNICATE IN CREATIVE WAYS

Learn to share your views in different ways. Use stories, facts, humor, and passion to convey your point. Do not let others discredit you because they can predict how you will express yourself every time.

In communicating your vision, be passionate, but learn to share that passion in different ways. Sometimes, convey your point with a story. Other times, relay your message using data and facts. Still other times, share a story or ask a question. Finally, consider using an appropriate joke to make your message more palatable to an audience. When your communication style becomes predictable, people may begin to discount what you have to say.

As a passionate person, I often employed fervent pleas and zealous appeals to spur others to action. Once, I needed campus administrators to understand how desperately we needed additional advisors to serve nursing students in the Counseling and Advising Center. In one team meeting, I repeatedly and emphatically stated that we simply must have more counselors for the nursing program. Afterwards, one of the counselors suggested that I share facts about the situation and find a variety of ways to explain the need. Her advice opened up a whole new line of communication for me. At the next meeting, I shared clear data, illustrating the high volume of nursing students coming through our center each day. Additionally, the story of one nursing student who waited many hours for advising vividly illustrated the need for additional staffing in our fast-growing nursing program. These varied approaches to communication produced results where my frequent, passionate pleas had failed.

Communicating in a variety of ways aided others in understanding the urgency of my problem and moved them to action. I carried an important lesson with me from that situation: Diversity of presentation makes for effective communication. Furthermore, I worked to become more creative in communicating my broader message and vision. This single principle revolutionized my style of communication. Oral presentations, written communication, thematic slogans, theatrical presentations, electronic messages, and leadership training all present opportunities for creative communication. Influential leaders use these mediums to lead and inspire.

#30

STRUCTURE TEAMS INTENTIONALLY

Structure teams so that they connect to the goals and objectives of your organization. Select strong leaders, and ensure the team is composed of individuals who bring the diverse skill sets needed to accomplish the team's goals.

One year, a major goal for our campus revolved around community partnerships. We purposely sought involvement with community partners to benefit both the college and the community. Our president first developed this goal, selecting dynamic leaders to serve as chairpersons for the team. Moreover, she spent time discussing her expectations with them to define clear, measurable outcomes for the initiative. Later, the chairpersons explained these things to the implementation team. The team made some modifications to these objectives and collaborated to develop methods for accomplishing the goal and measuring success.

In selecting the team, the chairpersons chose members to fill a variety of needs. A well-balanced team includes members who each bring certain vital skill sets. Of course, such a team requires members with specific knowledge and experience related to the team's task. The team should also include "idea people" who contribute creative energy to the group. Additionally, teams must involve people who pay attention to details, as well as those who can execute and complete the plan. Furthermore, someone who can sell ideas is imperative to any team, since these individuals normally perceive the way specific actions will impact others. Finally, at least one team member must possess strong communication skills. When teams are intentionally composed with these important skills in mind, the group will produce effective results for the organization.

#31

IDENTIFY THE INFLUENCERS

When new to an organization, identify ten people who influence the group in key ways. Get to know them. Share your dreams for the organization, and then ask for their assistance to make these dreams a reality.

One leader shared a crucial piece of advice when I was new to Brookhaven College. In seeking to build a strong leadership and student government program, she suggested identifying ten people who significantly influenced student life at the college. She further advised scheduling time for discussion with each of these people. By engaging these strategically selected people of influence, I could share my vision for the program, while presenting goals, objectives, and methods to accomplish them. In following her advice, I devised a series of questions to gather feedback from each of these people. After this series of meetings, the information I collected helped to reshape my goals and expectations for the program.

In the next stage of my efforts, I enlisted these ten influential leaders to help me build the program. With their help, we moved the plan forward. Through this approach, I led an initiative that resulted in a new leadership class to strengthen the student government program.

Influential faculty members, whom I initially identified and interviewed, became so excited about this new class that they helped promote it to students, recruiting the inaugural leadership class. My efforts to engage influential leaders in this endeavor worked to successfully secure buy-in from key supporters. When people of influence help conceive and design programs, leaders garner the support and assistance they need to launch successful initiatives.

#32

MAKE CRITICISM CONSTRUCTIVE

Provide constructive criticism by leading with positive affirmation. Begin any kind of correction by first pointing out all that has been completed in an excellent or satisfactory manner. Always follow constructive criticism with encouragement.

In working with a particular team, I needed to share how they had failed to complete a certain assignment with excellence. This critique was important, since I wanted the group to adopt high standards for the work which lay ahead. The group had put forth a great deal of effort; they simply did not reach the intended goal. Having a direct communication style, I simply shared the shortcomings of their work. Unfortunately, my approach deflated the enthusiasm of the entire team. Individuals at the meeting felt that their hard work went unappreciated. One mentor later shared an important insight with me. By launching into a list of perceived failures, my response created fear within the group. This fear would hinder the group's work, especially when a task required individuals to think boldly and take risks. Furthermore, the group might cease to cooperate effectively if individuals felt they needed to protect themselves from the consequences of possible failures in the future.

Looking back, I needed to realize that sometimes teams miss the mark in achieving their goals, despite their best efforts. Moreover, my mentor once imparted wise advice regarding the offering of criticism. To make criticism constructive, begin with the positive. Emphasize even small successes and point out things that went well in the process. Only after leading with the positive should leaders engage the group in discussing failed efforts and things that went wrong. Guide the group to list things they can do differently, so that a more successful outcome occurs when they resume their work. Share relevant data and statistics with the group to help them evaluate their efforts. Finally, encourage team members to stay involved as the team moves forward to accomplish its purpose. In this way, you can motivate them to continue pursuing the goal, by drawing on each other's strengths and working together.

#33

THE CHURCH IS THE WORLD

God expects Christians to live daily as models of His love and grace by responding to the needs of others. The people He places in our paths each day are part of our assignment. We grow His church any place and any time we encounter and serve such people.

During this season of my Christian growth, I struggled to find balance in my life when it came to God through the local church. From the time I could toddle through the church doors, service was ingrained in me as an important value. Now, with burgeoning career responsibilities, hours to serve the church became scarcer. This lack of time distressed me, and even after much prayer and thinking, no workable solution seemed to present itself.

At the time, I had a special relationship with the pastor of my church. As we talked one day, I explained to him the pressure I felt to serve the community, the church, my employer, and my family. After sharing my anguish with him, he said something I will never forget. He encouraged me to think of the world as the church and to simply do what God was leading me to do, even if it led me outside the church walls. For many years, I pondered what this meant. The concept was a confusing one for me, since I liked clearly defined tasks and roles. The blurring of lines between the church, my community, my family, and my job left me feeling unsure and unsteady. I wrestled with God to hear clearly from Him about when to engage in service and when to step aside.

Over the years, through much prayer and meditation, God has revealed a stronger sense of what this advice means. Instead of simply checking off acts of service in various categories, I now truly listen for God's guiding voice as I approach opportunities to serve others. This listening and doing is a more difficult, but more rewarding, kind of service. In it, I truly know God is using me for His unique purposes. As I listen for and obey His voice, I share His light and His love with the people He calls me to serve. Some of these people will never cross the threshold of a church building. Still, I am able to model Christ to them, because I am willing to serve where God leads me. Admittedly, I still struggle to fully embrace this concept, but it has surely changed my view of the world.

ECHOES FROM THE BROOKHAVEN YEARS

- **Work hard**. *As a leader, do not be afraid to do any task that is needed. Be willing to work alongside of others in the organization as you model a superb work ethics.*

- **Speak up.** *State what you know to be true even when others oppose your ideas. Always be true to what you believe.*

- **Learn to say no.** *Avoid accepting a new task if it means a job will not be done well. You may decide to drop one thing in order to accept a new task if it seems important.*

- **Listen deeply.** *Suspend your own internal thoughts when listening to the words of others. Listen to understand others. Remember that listening is fundamental to both understanding and being understood by others.*

- **Seek to understand others.** *Engage others in discussing their history and values, as you listen and learn their core values. This exchange will aid in forming strong working relationships.*

- **Look to God for guidance (Proverbs 3:5-6)**. *He will make your pathway clear.*

- **Learn to integrate all areas of your life.** *Place them under God's authority. Don't separate the various aspects of your life, but think of life as one continuous circle, with God at the center.*

- **Talk to God honestly.** *Be truthful with Him about your problems and concerns. Trust him, waiting patiently for Him to act. Count on Him to solve problems in His own way and on His time schedule.*

- **Surrender to God.** *Bring all phases of your life under His control. Allow Him to become the savior and master of your life.*

CHAPTER SEVEN

THE LANSING YEARS

"Leadership is best learned in the trenches."
—*Maria Angela Capello*

After more than ten years in the Dallas County Community College system, our family moved to Lansing, Michigan, as I became Dean of Student and Academic Support Divisions at Lansing Community College (LCC). The position was equivalent to a vice-president at other community colleges. Upon arrival, my responsibilities included leading the traditional student services units, along with the Multicultural Center and the Women's Resource Center. Additionally, the library, the radio and television stations, and online instruction fell under my purview, as well as developmental reading, writing, math, and science services. The move to Lansing was more than a professional and geographical relocation. In my new place of employment, I encountered a different kind of work culture. Lansing Community College functioned within an entirely different organizational framework than Brookhaven. While the Dallas County

Community College District functioned as a group of affiliated campuses, LCC operated as a single campus connected to the state system. Furthermore, the change meant moving from a non-union system to a union system. These circumstances presented unique challenges and opportunities. Wise executive leaders helped me navigated these new waters, and God faithfully continued to order my steps.

Approximately seven years after becoming dean, LCC elevated me to the position of Interim Provost and Chief Academic Officer. At the time, multiple changes were happening in the executive leadership of the college. This interim position unexpectedly turned into a three-year tenure, when administrators requested I remain as Provost to keep a sense of stability throughout the transition. As Provost, I acquired advanced leadership skills under the guidance of new mentors who helped me grow beyond my Brookhaven experience. One president at Lansing became a valuable mentor, as he recognized my talents, skills, and abilities. In his office one day, he encouraged me to enter a Ph.D. program. He explained that such a degree would add to my educational experience and open new doors in my career. His suggestion of someday becoming a community college president made me balk. The time required to be a working mother, wife, and student seemed an insurmountable obstacle. Upon serious reflection and significant prayer, however, my attitude toward the idea began to shift. A doctoral degree had never been my goal, but during this season at Lansing, I decided to pursue it. With my husband's blessing, I entered Michigan State University as a doctoral student.

In Michigan State's School of Education, classes took a variety of forms to benefit adult learners. These unique approaches to coursework helped me succeed as a working mother, wife, and executive leader. Intensive three-week courses and on-line courses with face-to face meetings connected my learning to real life experiences. Additionally, evening and week-end classes enabled me to continue working while maintaining my executive role at LCC. Each semester, I took a traditional face-to-face class, alongside one course in a nontraditional format. These methods proved to be strong tools for learning, while also providing needed flexibility. Moreover, this approach linked scholarly study at Michigan State to professional experiences at LCC, thus connecting work and school. Insights from my time as an adult learner impacted all of my future thinking and decisions related to such programs at the community college level.

Executive leaders at LCC firmly supported community involvement, because they saw the college as a resource for the community. They desired for the college's facilities, programs, administrators, faculty, and staff to add value to the communities we served. For example, the theatre and music departments offered opportunities for the community to partake in the arts. Furthermore, faculty members loaned their expertise to address community issues and problems. Additionally, the executive team encouraged campus leaders like me to serve as board members for local civic organizations. The team also valued active participation in community-wide initiatives. In this way, the community became a vital part of the college, truly bringing the community college to life through intentional engagement with our neighbors.

During these busy years, self-care and time-management emerged as critical components of my ability to sustain my family and my job in ways that brought deep satisfaction. Acting on some advice from several godly women in my church, I developed a time management plan according to my core values. In assessing my schedule, key priorities became apparent, including God, family, and work, and my own personal needs. Taking an honest look at things, it was obvious that my job consumed more time than desirable. Realizing the importance of balance, one of the first things I did was heed the counsel of a wise woman I knew. She recommended, "Give away tasks that add no value to your family." Her words led me to hire someone to do my housework and other household jobs. Another scheduling adjustment involved rising to pray early each day and combining this with an early morning exercise routine. Additionally, I carved out some weekly time for myself and my family, inviting my family to join me in activities like racquetball. Incorporating such changes in my life resulted in a sense of balance and peace that had been lacking.

Living and learning in Lansing, Michigan filled this period of life with joy and pride. I began to truly understand that life was a journey—a process full of experiences which built on one another to form a complete person. During these years, Jeremiah 29:11 (*NIV*) rang true in my life: "'For I know the plans I have for you,' declares the Lord, 'plans to prosper you and not to harm you, plans to give you hope and a future.'" Indeed, God had a plan for me, and the experiences He crafted for me fit together just as He designed. People, situations, jobs, communities—He was working all things together for my good (Romans 8:28, *NIV*). Looking back, I truly thank God for the people of Lansing, Michigan, to whom I owe a great deal.

LESSONS
LEARNED

from the Lansing Years

#34
DEVELOP COMMUNITY PARTNERSHIPS

Seek partnerships and systems for engaging the communities you serve. Develop structured ways for individuals in your organization to participate in community projects, so that both the community and the organization benefit.

Two presidents at LCC demonstrated the importance of community involvement, by engaging with community leaders to develop relationships and work together for the common good. This partnership required the creation and implementation of systematic approaches to community engagement. Wise leaders selected community projects carefully, knowing that such collaborations might not always directly benefit the organization but are critical to the community. One president directed efforts of the executive team by asking us to identify areas of the community that connected to the goals of the college. Additionally, the president requested that we pinpoint those community entities that most needed our participation in order to reach their goals. Once this list was developed, we were asked to select and share with him our plan for service. This process allowed each of us to serve key parts of the community without duplication of effort.

Among our executive team, interactions with many community members led to lifelong relationships. Such personal connections contributed to the accomplishments of both the college and the community. For example, work with one of the local ministers resulted in an effective program for the area's homeless. The project also benefitted the college in that participants eventually enrolled in college courses. The initiative, called *Stepping Stones*, revolved around gathering resources for the homeless in a single apartment complex. In doing this work, relevant community organizations provided centralized support for the homeless in one location. Some groups provided toiletries and other necessities, while LCC employees developed programs like summer camps for children in this place. Serving the community's children in this way inspired our team members, because it represented an investment in the future. At *Stepping Stones,* I realized how deeply I loved the work of community engagement and partnerships like this one.

#35

ESTABLISH EXPECTED OUTCOMES

Charter teams so that individuals know the expected outcomes for the work and are clear about expectations and lines of authority.

L ansing utilized teams to solve problems and accomplish many of the college's desired goals. At first, I often demonstrated a lack of patience with this lengthy process. LCC insisted every new team establish a specific charter. The charter required the team to define its purpose, outline expected outcomes, and clearly identify actions the team would and would not take to accomplish its goals. Additionally, the charter identified what the team could and could not do. For example, an executive might instruct the team to research best practices. On the other hand, the team might not be empowered to spend money. Moreover, the team must establish clear lines of authority. This distinction usually meant that the group would advise an executive leader on a matter for his or her consideration, but the group members would not be the final decision-makers. While an executive leader might empower a team to make decisions about some matters, such instances would be clearly outlined by the team's charter. These chartering procedures ensured that teams knew their stated purposes.

Chartering also required the team to develop expected outcomes and a plan of action that included a timeline. This organizing guided the team as they worked to implement their plan. Additionally, the charter articulated methods of evaluation to conclude if the team's work met expectations. At the end of the chartering process, the team reviewed the charter and sometimes used feedback to modify it. Once the charter was complete, teams began their work.

Constructing a charter involved painstaking work, but I learned to embrace it. Participating in this process at Lansing helped me grasp the importance of chartering teams that clearly establish expected outcomes. This establishing expectations and outcomes kept the team focused on their work and anchored to the college's strategic goals. My initial impatience with the process faded as I experienced the effective results of these carefully chartered teams.

#36

PREPARE FOR CHANGE

Prepare your organization for change by defining your strategy for necessary transitions. Clearly identify desired outcomes and methods to accommodate changes in the organization. Consider using a consultant for large efforts.

A t times, organizations must make comprehensive changes throughout their institution. While I had previously participated in some organizational restructuring, I had never led sweeping changes as a member of the executive leadership team. During the Lansing years, I acquired the knowledge to successfully lead such efforts. Prior to my arrival, the college had gone through a major reorganization that ignited large-scale efforts to implement changes throughout the campus. For instance, the college consolidated eight separate departments into five distinctly new divisions. In appointing leaders for these newly established divisions, some supervisors found their roles changed. Restructuring meant that some leaders began reporting to people they had previously supervised. For example,

129

several women in my department supervised separate areas in the college. After restructuring, this group functioned as a single leadership team. Also, the developmental reading, writing, and math programs moved from their individual academic departments to become one program, combining both academic and student services in order to support the whole student. Like the groups mentioned above, many of the campus employees found themselves working for unfamiliar supervisors in this new system.

Insightful executive leaders facilitated my learning about change management. Through their guidance, the college utilized professional consultants to direct the campus through the transition. One particular consultant spent time describing the critical role she would play in our college's transition efforts. She explained that her work included training other leaders in the college to eventually do her work. These trained campus leaders then assisted with professional development for the entire college. Through this approach, the consultant's efforts became campus-led initiatives. Moreover, the executive leadership team ensured that all employee groups took part in professional development, guaranteeing that desired changes filtered into every part of the organization. By learning how to lead large groups through complex change, I became well-equipped for future leadership opportunities.

#37

CREATE A CONTINUOUS IMPROVEMENT PLAN

Ensure your organization has a continuous improvement plan. Engage individuals throughout your organization by training them to look at data in order to continuously improve systems. Bring in experts to lead such training.

Lansing provided excellent training on continuous quality improvement. David P. Langford, who was once an educator, applied learning principles to this process. Some of the key concepts of David Langford could be summarized as the understanding that it is important to apply a systematic approach to improvement, as a way to both design and evaluate, as we create processes that exceed societal expectations.[5]

This type of systemic thinking proved especially valuable to me when I led a major effort to implement an updated registration process. A team worked to review the current system, identifying areas

131

JENNIFER WIMBISH, PH.D.

for improvement. Using Langford's approach resulted in many positive changes. For example, we devised a more efficient and effective way to deliver services in the financial aid office. In later years, LCC created an entire office devoted to quality improvement throughout the campus. Individuals in this office worked across all departments to improve many of the college's essential systems and processes. Exposure to this kind of continuous quality improvement aided me when I later became a community college president.

#38

LEAD THE WAY

Great teachers lead the way. They support students by responding to their personal needs.

The Michigan State University doctoral program was led by master professors, who modeled caring and personalized instruction. Their example impacted my view of leading and teaching in significant ways. Professors in my program facilitated learning by spending quality time with students, in order to better understand and respond to their needs as adult learners. For example, during a difficult time of research related to the dissertation, one instructor decided to have some of our class meet weekly in his home, instead of on campus. This relaxed, comfortable environment benefited the members of our small class. As the professor instructed us about the best way to complete the research and dissertation process, this intimate atmosphere enhanced the learning process. On another occasion, I recall one of my instructors returning a paper to me during my lunch hour at work. He had a meeting near my workplace, so he took time to hand deliver my paper, because he wanted me to receive useful feedback on that assignment before beginning the next one.

These were not the only examples of instructors who modeled caring and personalized instruction. One key individual in my doctoral studies exhibited exceptional instructional leadership. After two years on my dissertation committee, she accepted a different position at another university. She was also a part of the dissertation committee for two other students in my class. She modeled real concern for our success, by working with the education department to participate on our committees when we defended our dissertations. Looking back, this professor's presence and support clearly contributed to the successful defense of our dissertations. Actions like these were rooted in genuine, student-centered learning, and they shaped my thinking as a college administrator. In all future professional roles, I strived to follow this pattern of behavior.

#39

DEVELOP COLLABORATIVE EFFORTS

Make sure your work is efficient and cost effective by joining with other organizations to complete large initiatives. When appropriate, connect to like-minded organizations at the state, national, and international level.

Community colleges in Michigan often worked with other colleges throughout the state on major initiatives. This differed from my experiences in Texas. Once, for example, dozens of colleges came together to institute new instructional programs that the state deemed important to its economic development. Instead of duplicating the same effort at each college, several colleges worked together to devise a curriculum every campus could utilize for these new programs. In another instance, colleges from across the state decided to sponsor specialized training for all campuses in the same location. State sponsored training from the Disney corporation benefitted student services professionals from colleges throughout Michigan. The cost of this extraordinary training could have exceeded the budget of a single college. By streamlining training efforts for several colleges at once, however, it became an affordable option.

At LCC, such streamlined efforts between colleges led to more collaborative thinking about partnerships in the community. Coordinating efforts between the college, school system, churches, and youth organizations maximized resources for all of these groups. In one case, these entities cooperated to develop a program to support males who desired to complete high school and advance to college. In cooperating, they leveraged their joint resources for the common good of the community. By observing collaborative programs of this nature, I became aware that such planning and implementation promoted efficacy and lowered costs. This foundational strategy to leading initiatives across large groups brought untold opportunities and successes.

#40

ASK GOOD QUESTIONS

Ask questions designed to aid understanding of the organiza-
tion's goals and challenges. As a supervisor, asking good questions
of your team members helps you uncover information, monitor
progress, and establish accountability.

I will never forget giving a report to one LCC president about an action I wanted to recommend. After hearing my report, he asked me a series of questions. He repeated one question several times: "*Why?*" I was not prepared to answer the question at any level. Later, he explained his use of a practice known as "the 5 *Whys*."[6] This approach, learned from Sakichi Toyoda's work at Toyota Motor Corporation, assisted him in uncovering the core reasons behind a leader's decision. Every time he asked the question, the response yielded a deeper reason, ultimately revealing a root belief behind the leader's thinking. Additionally, the president asked me questions designed to help him understand how my recommendation fit into the larger scheme of the college's goals. He also wanted to know specific outcomes and expectations for the project. Finally, he asked about methods for evaluating the initiative and ways to define success.

As our meeting ended, I voiced my observation that he always asked good questions about major initiatives for the college. The president responded by saying that strong executive leaders must ask questions to assist them in understanding the activities of their organization. "A single leader," he said, "cannot always know everything that occurs in a large institution, so he must ask questions." He further suggested developing a list of effective questions that may apply to any situation in the organization. Such practices, he asserted, created accountability when individuals learned to anticipate strong questions in advance. Establishing an expected line of questioning assisted leaders in effectively conceiving and designing college-wide efforts. This astute president clearly understood the role of strategic questions in training administrators to align initiatives with the college's goals and objectives.

#41

KNOW WHEN TO LEAVE

Take time to evaluate your work in the organization, leaving for your next position on your own terms. When 51% or more of the people in an organization do not support your work, consider that it may be time to leave. A job becomes more difficult when more than one-half of the people work against you.

K now when it is time to move to a new position or to retire. Once, a colleague wanted to move forward with new concepts and ideas for the college. Unfortunately, many individuals in the organization did not support her work. In speaking with the campus president about this dilemma, he offered some poignant advice. He insisted, "Jennifer, someday you will most likely be president of a college. In this situation, it will be important for you to know when it is time to leave an institution and seek your next position." He continued, "You are passionate about your work; however, there are some things you should consider. Be wise and learn to leave when you have completed the work and done a good job. You want to leave when things are in good shape. You do not want to stay too long and leave because your support has waned. Be sure to listen to the voices of the people in the organization. This is a difficult task, especially when you are leading an organization and are passionate about the work you want to do. But it is essential for every executive to do this. I have often seen people fail to do this and create a situation that is not good for anyone."

The president further concluded that when 51% of the people are against your efforts, it is time to leave. "Without majority support," he quipped, "you lose when you lose, and you lose when you win." He believed that simply being passionate about your work did not always mean you should stay. The work is often difficult and only becomes harder without the backing of others. Sometimes, it is best to leave, because it will be too tough to turn things around and make a positive impact. Additionally, the president advised that if your supervisor does not lead in a direction consistent with your core values, it is likely time to go. Finally, he noted that sometimes you simply must leave because a new leader comes on board. Many times, a newly appointed leader desires a fresh team to administer his or her unique vision. Top officials deserve the opportunity to build their own team. "If you have done good work," he encouraged, "you will know that you can always find a new position."

As I approached retirement, I also learned that you must listen to the voice of God in such decisions. Also, you must realize it is time to go when you no longer have the drive and energy required for the job. These signs often indicate it is time to move on to another phase of life. Through such reflection, observations, and advice, I determined that finishing well meant exercising the wisdom to leave an organization gracefully.

ECHOES FROM THE LANSING YEARS

- **Value every employee group**. *In leading your organization, provide professional opportunities for everyone.*
- **Insist on unity**. *Leaders may debate issues behind closed doors, but once a decision is reached, the entire team must present unified communication in support of organization.*
- **Write down your reasons**. *When sharing important decisions, write out your rationale, supporting your position in a one-minute presentation. This will sharpen your thinking about the matter.*
- **Successful groups efforts require strong facilitation**. *Appoint well-trained facilitators to preside over meetings. Provide opportunities for those interested in this work to receive necessary training. Every organization needs gifted and well-trained facilitators.*
- **Begin the day with God.** *Diligently seek Him with your whole heart throughout the entire day. He is sure to speak when you do.*
- **Seek Christian mentors.** *Let God lead you to talented and gifted individuals who can enrich your life.*
- **Know what speaks to your soul.** *Include these practices in your devotional time. For example, if music moves you, find ways to incorporate*

it into spiritual routines. Seek Godly friends who have your same beliefs and include them in your friendships.

- **Be still.** *Stop speaking, get quiet, and listen to God's voice as He directs your path.*

PART THREE

LEGACY

CHAPTER EIGHT

THE PARENTING YEARS

Mothers are the rocks of our families and a foundation in our communities. In gratitude for their generous love, patient counsel, and lifelong support let up pay respect to women who carry out the work of motherhood with skill and grace and let us remember those who, though are no longer with us, inspire us still.

—Barack H. Obama

Life shifted when Michael and I welcomed our one and only son, Michael Wimbish, Jr., in 1984. After his arrival, we briefly entertained the idea of me being a stay-at-home mom. Three months later, we prayerfully agreed on my return to the professional world. This transition required keen time-management skills to ensure proper care of our growing family and myself. New challenges loomed in order to balance expanding roles of mother, wife, daughter, sister, and career woman. With this balance in mind, I actively searched for seminars designed to equip and encourage working mothers. My parents and in-laws also shaped my thoughts about parenting. Additionally, successful career women whom I interviewed—including Christian women— helped prepare me for this new journey.

While I quickly fell in love with parenting, it demanded constant time, energy, and prayer. Learning from other effective Christian parents became a priority for me. As a new mother—and throughout the years—conversations with strong role-models like parents and in-laws shaped and influenced my parenting. Prayer also proved an essential part of parenting, as devotions included time to ask the Lord for wisdom in raising our son. Furthermore, Bible study included a new emphasis on what God's word said about parenting. Often, God guided me through heartfelt conversations with other Christian mothers who shared powerful insight.

When Michael, Jr. was ten, I accepted a position at Lansing Community College as a Dean of Student and Academic Support Divisions. This position represented a major career advancement and moved our family from Dallas, Texas to Lansing, Michigan. At the time, my fifth-grade son did not welcome this change. He deeply resented us for taking him away from his school and his friends. In fact, after learning about the move, he insisted on a family vote before we made a final decision. Relocating was initially difficult, especially as my husband commuted between Dallas and Lansing weekly. He came on Thursday night and left early Tuesday morning, splitting time between the two cities for four days each week. While it took time to adjust to these changes, we dedicated ourselves to spending quality family time with our son the other three days a week. In time, Michael, Jr. grew to love his new home, school, and friends. During these years, valuable concepts presented by his principal, teachers, and other mature Christian women assisted me greatly. Their strong advice taught me to seek out support, manage my time, and stay connected to God throughout these critical parenting years.

As my son grew into a teenager, I again sought wisdom from mothers who successfully raised well-educated children. Christian women with healthy families and thriving children enthusiastically shared the methods they used in training up their sons and daughters. Such interactions began an on-going dialogue about parenting, which led to some intentional lifestyle changes for our family. While many wise men and fathers offered important counsel, too, it was the thinking of women that most shaped my decisions. Moreover, time with God provided divine guidance as I sought to become an effective working mother. Taking these steps along the parenting journey allowed me to enjoy both motherhood and my career.

LESSONS
LEARNED

from the Parenting Years

#42

GIVE AWAY NON-ESSENTIAL TASKS

Give away those things that add no value to family life. Seek help from grandparents and friends who want to support your family. Learn to hire individuals who can do task that are not important for you to do.

O ne day, during a conversation with my mother about child rearing, she shared the importance of having someone in the home to support the mother and care for the child during his infant years. This meant the child's daily routine stayed as consistent as possible, while the parent worked away from home. In performing these duties for another woman, she observed how the arrangement reduced stress in the family. I recalled this conversation at a time when balancing motherhood and a career felt particularly overwhelming. Applying her wise advice, my husband and I found a wonderful woman who was an experienced mother to care for our son at home during the first three years of his life. While she primarily cared for our son, in a few cases she assisted with other household chores. Later, this trusted woman guided us to see that, as an only child, our son would benefit from enrolling in an early childhood education program where he could socialize with other children. This instance was not the only time God guided us to someone who assisted in this kind of role.

During the Lansing years, God spoke directly to my heart in church one Sunday. Sitting in the pew, pondering over who might be able to pick up my son from school, God told me to speak with the senior high school Sunday school teacher about this matter. At the end of the service, I forgot to reach out to the teacher. A voice said to me, "Did I not tell you to talk to the Sunday school teacher before you leave today?" When I returned to ask this woman about a high school student who could potentially bring Michael, Jr. home from school each day, her answer shocked me. She emphatically responded, "Why not have me do it?" With a small budget for this job, I assumed that we could not pay enough to employ someone with her qualifications. This mature, retired Christian lady had many years of experience serving youth. After expressing my concerns, she kindly responded, "Working with children and senior citizens is a gift given from God that I want to share with you and your family. I can work for what you can afford." After welcoming her into our home and lives for five years, I realized that no amount of money we paid her could ever truly compensate for the guidance and encouragement she provided all of us. God truly blessed our family through her in ways that can never be repaid.

#43

SEEK SUPPORT SYSTEMS

Partner with like-minded families and community organizations to help meet the needs of your child. In the teen years, select a college student to help with homework and mentor your child.

Join forces with other families to support each other in parenting tasks. Share the load when it comes to transportation to extracurricular and church activities. Additionally, consider organizing a parent's network, collaboratively partnering to create solutions to common problems. Furthermore, seek to develop a back-up plan for times when meetings run late or children get sick. Always have someone who can assist your child or attend events in your absence. Consider grandparents, neighbors, retired friends, college students, and individuals from your church to fill this role, making sure they share your family's values. For the sake of consistency, strive to select one or two individuals who regularly help with these tasks. In doing these things, you will create a village of resources for your son or daughter.

Additionally, utilize community resources to help support your child. For example, when my son was in elementary school, several

African American mothers wanted their children to learn more about Black history and culture. We worked with the local community college to establish a monthly program to meet this need. In the same way, neighborhood families united to create a Spanish course taught by a well-respected instructor. Another time, the local library held a weeklong summer camp for African American students. Look for similar ways your community can offer support.

Also, look for young adults who share your values to mentor your child. Especially in the high school years, consider recruiting a college student to expose your child to the college environment and to assist with difficult homework assignments. A professor at Lansing Community College suggested I find this kind of role model for my son. She expressed how important it was for my son to have a successful young role model encouraging him in academics and college preparations. This need for mentorship proved especially true for young African American boys in our community.

A student from the local university spent two afternoons each week with Michael, Jr. This mentor introduced my son to all the fun, positive aspects of university life, helping Michael see college as a desirable goal. Additionally, he stressed the importance of earning good grades in high school and assisted our son with difficult homework assignments. When the young man arrived, one of the first things he did was to burn my son's favorite music on the computer. This was exciting for Michael and allowed him to quickly connect with this young man. I learned to treasure this unique mentoring arrangement, for it assisted our family not only with difficult homework assignments but also with having someone in the home who could identity with Michael and point him in the right direction. Support systems like this one made all the difference for our son.

#44

EQUIP YOUR CHILD TO MAKE DECISIONS

Teach your child a decision-making strategy, giving him or her clear methods for solving problems. This skill is foundational in order for your child to gain independence. Such skills empower him or her to exercise personal responsibility in response to life's daily challenges.

In raising children, remember that you are preparing your child to function as an adult. As such, your child must not always depend on you to do everything for him or her. Children must learn to navigate problems and make wise decisions on their own; this is the goal of strong parenting. Equip your children by teaching them an effective model for making important choices. The following model helped my son discover how to make solid decisions.[7]

- **Define the Problem.** *Evaluate and clearly state the problem that needs solving.*

- **Whose problem is it?** *Determine if it is truly your responsibility to solve this problem.*

- **If the problem is not yours, give it away.** *Consider whether a teacher, parent, or employer needs to handle the problem.*

- **Write down several possible solutions.** *Think of four or five workable solutions to address the problem.*

- **Weigh the options.** *Rate the options on a scale of 1-10.*

- **Rank the solutions.** *Rank the solutions from most desirable to least desirable, according to your personal values.*

- **Choose a response.** *Discuss the options with yourself. Then make a choice.*

- **Do not look back.** *Once the decision has been made, move quickly to act.*

#45

PAVE THE WAY FOR TRANSITIONS

When a child's life is interrupted by significant change, formulate a strategic plan to help the child navigate the transition smoothly. Relocation, divorce, or death are all situations requiring an intentional response.

Our family resolved not to make major life changes after our son entered fifth grade. If at all possible, we did not want him to endure major transitions in middle or high school. While this was our ideal scenario, life does not always turn out according to plan. Sometimes, changes occur whether we want them or not. When major disruptions do occur in your child's life, wise parenting can lead them through uncertain times. For example, in moving to a new town, your child will need to change schools and make new friends. A strong plan for a smooth transition can pave the way for your son or daughter.

When relocating, think ahead. For example, a former principal suggested we find three or four families with similar family values and engage in activities with them before school started. Planning social activities beforehand allowed our son to embark on his first day of school with friends who helped to introduce him to others. Their assistance helped him adjust more smoothly. Additionally, conversations with teachers and school administrators before our son enrolled helped them understand the educational goals and expectations we had for our son. These professionals then assisted us in constructing an appropriate educational experience. During the first weeks in the new environment, they also recommended I enlist someone to observe my son and share updates on how he was adapting. We also invited my parents to spend vacation time with us during the transition, so they could provide feedback on our son's transition, too. This network allowed me to address issues and concerns immediately. Furthermore, in order to build a sense of belonging in our new community, we engaged in church related and local events early in our relocation. In following the sound advice of teachers and school administrators, my husband and I made the transition as smooth as possible for our son.

#46

HAVE ESSENTIAL CONVERSATIONS

Define a designated time to check in with your child on a regular basis. Do not avoid difficult conversations. If you do not talk to your child about essential matters, they will listen to someone else who may not hold your values.

E stablish open lines of communication with your child by talking with him or her regularly. For young children, parents can easily incorporate these conversations into a bedtime routine along with prayer. When my son entered elementary school, I found the travel time to school each morning was a perfect time for focused conversation. One parent I know encouraged conversation in the car by turning off the radio and forbidding the use of electronics. This eliminated distractions while she engaged her children in conversation while driving. The daily commute to school and to extra-curricular activities often provided a consistent time to talk about a variety of things, from silly to serious.

As my son became a teen, I continued to have daily communication with him in order to stay in tune with his life. Our weekly racquetball games afforded a relaxed setting to have important conversations. I never shied away from difficult subjects. I followed my mother's example in having frank, age-appropriate discussions about sex. These talks gave me the opportunity to convey what the Bible teaches about male and female relationships. Moreover, we also talked over the characteristics of healthy friendships. Often, when hard things happened in my son's world, our time together created a safe space to communicate. I cherished every opportunity to speak into his life—in the big things and in the little things.

#47

SET THE TONE IN YOUR HOME

Rise early in the morning before your family to spend time in prayer and devotion to God. In this way, you set the tone for the day as God leads. Moreover, this time prepares you to move through the day with the peace only God provides.

Many Christian women remember the description of a godly woman in Proverbs 31. The Bible describes her as "a wife of noble character"[1] (Proverbs 31:10, *NIV*), rising while it was yet night to prepare for the next day.

Once, I attended a workshop that thoroughly examined this example from scripture. In explaining the Proverbs 31 woman, the speaker explained that these verses indeed describe a working woman. She further noted that this woman rose early in the morning to establish the desired tone for her family and to cook daily provisions for them. Extending this challenge to the women in her audience, the speaker admonished us to rise earlier than anyone else in our homes to spend special time alone with God. Through practicing this habit, the godly woman had found it to bring peace to both her and her family. As I accepted her challenge, I discovered her advice proved true. Even today, though often difficult, when I rise early for time with God, my entire day seems more peaceful. Even if my family awakens in a foul mood or the morning becomes chaotic, I do not react in kind. In this way, I set the tone for my family's day.

In addition to this practice, I observed that the Bible teaches that some things come only by fasting and praying[1] (Mark 9:29, *NIV*). Desiring my son to make Jesus Christ his Lord and Savior, I learned to fast and pray for him and for other family matters on a regular basis. As a parent, my husband and I also defined a weekly time on Sundays for worship, Bible study, and family devotion. These strategies helped set the tone for our home in more comprehensive ways.

#48

ENGAGE YOUR CHILD IN CHURCH

Engage your child in church as he develops his relationship with God. Participate in church activities alongside your son or daughter.

After my son was born, church involvement continued to play a vital role in our family's life. For my husband and me, having a small child meant selecting a church with a strong children's ministry. From this perspective, our son's needs became more important than our own when it came to finding a church. Our church placed major emphasis on its ministry to children, which included a licensed Christian daycare. This church's emphasis on the youth ensured that our son had opportunities early in his life to learn about God. Moreover, in order to be engaged with my son, I decided to work in the church nursery on Sundays. While this meant relinquishing some of my favorite church activities, it yielded rich fruit during this season of my life. My service in the children's ministry presented many chances to interact with experienced educators and mothers.

From them, I absorbed foundational knowledge about becoming a strong Christian parent.

Because our family treasured church and considered it a cornerstone for life, we did not allow church participation to wane during my son's busy teen years. Instead, my husband and I engaged with him in youth activities at the church. Once, when seeking to train our son to share his faith, we worked with youth leaders to create such a program. They welcomed our initiative to involve the youth in such training. In fact, our desire to teach our son to share his faith turned into a church-wide effort with the support of church leaders and staff members. Intentional engagement at church throughout our son's life paid lasting dividends, because it helped him cultivate a strong relationship with God.

ECHOES FROM THE PARENTING YEARS

- **Teach God's word.** *Help your child understand the Bible. Surround your family with others who embrace Christian beliefs.*
- **Utilize age-appropriate materials.** *Buy books, music, toys, and games that teach biblical truths. Ask your children's minster or a Christian teacher to help you generate a list of such resources.*
- **Establish clear educational goals.** *In assessing childcare, school, and church opportunities, select programs that align with your goals. Remember, every child has different needs.*
- **Attend parenting seminars.** *Seek out sessions that teach effective parenting methods at each stage of your child's life.*
- **Understand your child.** *Identify the individual personality, talents, skills, strengths, and weaknesses of your child at an early age. Connect to programs and individuals who can help develop these.*
- **Establish a reward system**. *Use this to acknowledge and reward positive behaviors, confronting serious behavior quickly.*
- **Help your child develop a strong self-esteem.** *Children need to feel they have intrinsic value and worth. Work to communicate these*

things. Spend time with them, kneel to look them in the eyes, sit near them, listen to them, and invite them to do things with you.

- **Expose your child to college**. *During the teen years, visit public, private, religious, and community colleges. When possible, incorporate college visits into fun family vacations.*

- **Promote financial literacy.** *Look for age-appropriate programs that teach saving and investment strategies. Consider having your family take a course like this to encourage future financial stability.*

- **Guide career choices.** *Teach resume-writing and interview skills. Look for internships and apprenticeships that will help your child discern future career goals.*

CHAPTER NINE

THE PRESIDENCY YEARS

In learning you will teach, and in teaching you will learn.

—Phil Collins

As I reached the pinnacle of my career, I assumed responsibilities as the president of Cedar Valley College (CVC) in August of 2003. This campus in Lancaster, Texas, became my professional home until my retirement in August of 2016. As one of the seven campuses of the Dallas County Community College District (DCCCD), Cedar Valley played a pivotal role early in my career. I was happy to return to a campus that brought me so much joy as a rising young professional. In many ways, accepting the position truly felt like coming home.

As president of Cedar Valley College, insightful leaders continued to inspire and coach me. However, it was during the early years of my presidency that I came to a poignant realization. The words of a dear cousin prompted the discovery that my role had now shifted from that of a ment*ee* to that of a ment*or* (who is continuing to learn). My cousin—an eminent historian and brilliant educator—often spoke profound truths into my life. In seeking his opinion during a conversation one day, he proclaimed, "Jennifer, you need to recognize that your time as a junior professional seeking advice from others has ended. You must embrace the fact that, as a professional, you have attained all the skills you need to mentor and assist others who follow behind you. You already know the answers to the questions that you have asked me. Now act upon them." Indeed, his words resonated deep inside me, moving me to gratefully welcome this new role. This position served as a significant turning point, and I resolved to prioritize mentoring others in the same ways that others had so blessed me.

Lessons from previous chapters represent the voices of exceptional leaders and a mighty God. In the following pages, I seek to join this great conversation by adding my voice to theirs. Striving to include unique character and leadership principles, I have drawn on my professional experiences, spiritual journey, and community involvement to draw conclusions about life that come from the depths of my heart and soul. These lessons in my own words relate to leadership, people, planning, and balance. While concepts presented here may refer to ideas from earlier chapters, the lessons that follow encompass my own unique knowledge and understanding.

MY REMARKS AND REFLECTIONS

GROWING IN LEADERSHIP

STAY CURRENT

The world is in a state of continuous change. This means leaders must remain current on local, state, national, and international matters. Study and review a diverse body of literature, while regularly listening to various media sources to discover all sides of an issue. Read authors with different viewpoints that challenge your initial thoughts on a topic. Additionally, engage in discussions with people from varied backgrounds when you attend professional conferences. Since you cannot become an expert on everything, focus your efforts to stay current on subjects connected to your individual purpose and life's work. Technology has also become a critical tool needed to stay abreast of our ever-evolving world, so utilize it to further your understanding of important matters. Even in retirement, I have discovered I must adapt to new technology. For example, writing this book pushed me to use new electronic methods for communication and document storage. While these things have challenged and even frustrated me, I realize that leaders must continue to learn if they want to stay relevant.

SURROUND YOURSELF WITH GREAT PEOPLE

Such people do not come along at every turn. Learn to recognize them and engage with them. These kinds of strong leaders share their thoughts with you, especially when they see you doing something that bears correcting. Hire great people like this in your part-time or temporary pool of employees. Their skilled leadership and years of experience will enhance all the members of your team. In a part-time or temporary capacity, these individuals can also guide others to accomplish large projects. Additionally, they are ideally suited to serve an organization while you are waiting to fill key vacancies on the staff. Once at Cedar Valley, we needed to hire a new executive team member. I had already hired someone whom I considered a great person to fill a temporary position in another part of the college. Because of this person's mature leadership and understanding of the college, this individual effectively preformed the executive duties of these two vacant positions, while we recruited the best candidate for each job. Surrounding yourself with great people like this allows your organization to benefit from their knowledge and expertise.

PUBLISH YOUR SUCCESSES

Write about successful initiatives implemented under your leadership. Publish those things, so that your peers may benefit by learning about your work. For example, recording effective strategies can save others from duplicating the work it took you to attain success. It may also keep them from duplicating mistakes you made along the way. Additionally, publish your organization's achievements as a way to celebrate the group's accomplishments. For example, a consultant who came to Cedar Valley noted the fine work of many employee groups on our campus. In touring the grounds, she adamantly urged, "You simply *must* write for various national, state, and local publications on the degree of success you are achieving here! Your college deserves this recognition, and so do your people. Writing about Cedar Valley's accomplishments will leave a legacy that others can learn from." While our team had presented programs and even won awards at national conventions, the thought of writing about such things took me by surprise. She further challenged me by saying, "A great work has been done at your college. But because you have not published it, I never realized until witnessing it on your campus today." Her recommendation echoed in my mind and always made me wish I had written more.

KEEP YOUR INTEGRITY INTACT

As a leader, always tell the truth. No matter how difficult it seems, practicing honesty can free the soul. Wisdom, however, must guide you in knowing *when* to speak truth. Often, it serves no good purpose to correct someone in the presence of others simply because you want to tell the truth. This public correcting can only cause embarrassment and resentment. Wise judgment dictates doing these kinds of things in private whenever possible. Other times, with colleagues whom you trust, you might deftly address the matter in front of others by stating, "I have a different understanding of this." Use "I" statements to share your perspective, in order to eliminate potentially hurtful accusations. I recall using a variation of this approach once in a meeting. Upon hearing something I suspected to be untrue, I addressed it by saying, "I want to be sure that I have a good grasp of this situation. Let me explain my understanding of things." This allowed me to state the things I believed were true in this situation.

Moreover, a person of integrity understands that honesty extends beyond words to include actions. Do not cover up your faults and errors. Learn to simply say in a respectful manner, "I made a mistake." Additionally, do not be afraid to ask for help. Furthermore, while honesty requires you to always *tell* the truth, you must also *act* in truthful, legal, moral, and ethically ways. Remember, what is legal is not always ethical. Know how to confront situations that make you uncomfortable on these levels. I devised a straightforward approach in cases that caused me discomfort on ethical grounds. I clearly stated, "This is an ethical issue for me; therefore, I need to share my thinking on the matter." Moreover, utilize legal counsel to advise on such cases. Doing these things will keep your integrity intact.

CONNECTING WITH PEOPLE

HONOR THE VALUES OF OTHERS

Strive to treat people both the way that *you* want to be treated and the way *they* want to be treated. As long as you can stay true to your own values, honor others in this way. Especially with people from different ethnicities, religions, and worldviews, this requires careful listening in order to discern what things they value most. Seek to respond to people's need in ways that support their beliefs, as long as it does not involve something unethical, illegal, or immoral. When conflicts arise, showing respect often paves the way to resolution. As a leader, be clear about your beliefs without demeaning those who disagree with you. Even so, do not avoid sharing your beliefs out of fear or intimidation; sharing your beliefs will enable others to better understand you. The world becomes stronger when people of all generations and backgrounds take time to know one another and learn together.

ENCOURAGE OTHERS TO GROW

Provide professional development and growth opportunities for all employee groups and for those that you serve. In the college, for example, include student employees and student learners in professional development experiences. Connect such training to the goals and objectives of the institution. Ensure training is offered through a variety of delivery methods, including online and mobile formats utilizing current technology. Consider that in-house training opportunities allow more individuals to participate in professional growth opportunities; however, also recognize occasions for relevant field trips and participation in off-campus meetings and conventions. One of the wisest approaches I know deliberately grows leaders from inside your organization to develop the leadership potential within your own ranks. For example, the human resources team suggested that I create a President's Leadership Academy at Cedar Valley to help identify and train leaders in the college who demonstrated an aptitude for becoming future administrators and executive leaders. In these monthly four-hour sessions, I focused on essential topics concerning our campus while getting to know rising leaders. Today, I continue to mentor and support some of these individuals. It is fulfilling to watch as they execute principles they learned in this program. Over the years, professional development has tugged at my heart, because it encompasses my passion to serve and encourage others. The rewards in performing this service for others have been immeasurable.

EMBRACE SERVANT LEADERSHIP

Impactful leaders focus on the needs of the people they serve. I heard someone say, "We should seek to be a blessing every day to someone." As I work with and speak to others, this principle undergirds all my efforts. When my day seems especially challenging, I simply find a way to bless someone else, and my entire attitude shifts. In leading others, this principle reminds me to emphasize issues that truly matter for people. This concept often results in joining others who passionately work to solve problems affecting large groups. In working with people, this principle leads me to reach out to individuals in ways that make a difference in their struggles. For example, throughout my career, I have treasured the opportunity to help students reach their goals. Whether it is on a large scale or a small scale, servant leadership has always been my goal.

While it is important for leaders to engage in solving social problems, it is also important to involve the people we seek to serve in processes. In this way, we can more accurately design systems to meet their needs. Often, I have observed leaders discuss an issue and decide how to respond. Many times, the projects and programs they create fail, because they do not address the true needs of the people they seek to serve. Instead, they address only the problems perceived by leaders. Once, in developing a plan to increase the number of students who graduated from our campus, we asked students to share their thoughts on the matter. We were somewhat surprised by their responses. While our plan addressed many things, we learned one thing students needed most was an easy way to speak directly to counselors and advisors in the registration process. Another time, in working to ensure that adult students felt comfortable coming to campus, we heard students share that they failed to enroll, because the campus seems too large and frightening. Some of these students indicated that they wanted to come register in person rather than on-line. To better serve prospective adult students, we recruited current adult students to call them personally and to walk them through the registration process on campus. These strategic changes centered on meeting the tangible needs of others.

Moreover, servant leaders have the responsibility to advocate for the powerless, by speaking truth to policies and systems that hurt the very people who most need assistance. For example, as I move around our country, I often meet people who work two or three jobs just to survive. In many of these instances, they still cannot afford to live a decent life, because their jobs do not pay a livable wage. Their plight moves me. Recently, I joined a community initiative that focuses on bringing more jobs with higher wages to our community. We also work to raise awareness of these opportunities and promote these employers in our local neighborhoods. This initiative is also seeking to create a collaborative workforce entity that assists underemployed individuals. Our efforts even extend to helping the homeless in locating the services they need to secure employment. We provide food, transportation, and childcare stipends to assist this process.

Furthermore, we utilize a data system to help homeless individuals locate affordable housing and a case management system to track individuals and support them throughout the job seeking process. Intervening to serve those with no resources—and no voice in society—achieves the highest goal of true servant leadership.

DEVELOPING A PLAN

THINK AND PLAN STRATEGICALLY

Engage your organization in strategic thinking connected to an aligned strategic plan. Make sure the mission (your purpose) and vision (future direction) of your organization are tied to specific goals and objectives. In other words, put your beliefs into action. Be sure to evaluate the efficiency and effectiveness of your actions by using data to measure your progress and your accomplishments. Leaders must call for reports that communicate these things to everyone in the organization. Such reports show where improvements are still needed. Additionally, be sure to tie employee reviews to goals and objectives within your strategic plan. Accountability systems like these prove critical to the success of any organization. Furthermore, a strong project management system must support the work of the college. A skilled project manager will gather data and use it to develop an accountability plan. Moreover, establish a communication dashboard to facilitate sharing such results. This level of feedback is necessary to encourage your team to think and plan strategically. Aligning your strategic plans to your thinking in this way means that members of your organization will become effectively engaged in the work of the college.

Use Your Vision to Paint a Picture

Make sure your vision provides a clear direction for the future and is easily understood by the individuals in your organization. Someone once told me that you can tell in five minutes if the vision of an organization is real to its members. To achieve this, use creative methods to clearly explain your plan and inspire others with your vision. For example, a picture or other artwork can make your vision come to life for people. Once at Cedar Valley, our executive team developed an exciting vision for the future of the college while attending a conference off-campus. We felt excited about our new vision statement: *"Cedar Valley College will become a community of leaders developing leaders through student success."* As we shared this vision upon returning to campus, people immediately wanted to know what this meant. We quickly realized more work lay ahead of us. Later, we assembled a team to refine our vision. While the team understood that words defined the vision in an important way, the team also labored to develop a vision statement that painted a vivid picture for people. In the end, the team used the image of a graduate travelling down life's path to a desired destination. Since students at Cedar Valley pursued various goals, these images portrayed destinations like urban workplaces and institutions of higher education. This visual helped individuals throughout the campus connect with the vision of our college, no matter their future plans. In picturing their own future, they fully grasped the vision of Cedar Valley College. Never underestimate the value of a single image to communicate a bigger idea.

Utilize Technology in Accessible Ways

Today, we live and learn in a technologically rich world. While leaders must include technology in any continuous improvement plan, it is vital to make sure all individuals can easily access technology. Remember that individuals from different backgrounds and generations may require assistance with these tools. Financial constraints can also create a technology divide, where those who most need the technology cannot afford it. When this is the case, partner with churches and community organizations to provide access to technology in a central location. If leaders fail to provide access, they risk leaving behind an entire segment of the population. For example, in working with a group of students and parents, I assumed everyone had a cell phone and could communicate by text. After the meeting, some individuals shared that they did own a cell phone. Some grandparents shared that they did not know how to text. For a period, we decided to continue sending postcards and letters through the mail. At the same time, we recruited some of the younger students to teach the older adults how to utilize text messaging. Since millennials and younger individuals grew up with technology, they can often help others who need to learn. In fact, one organization I know grants time away from the job for individuals to assist in this way, because the entire group benefits when individuals learn to use new systems of technology. While leaders can easily see the value in older adults sharing wisdom with younger generations, the reverse of that model can also yield dividends—especially when it comes to implementing technology.

Moreover, organizations must employ continuous improvement strategies to ensure that the technology works for the client in useful ways. This requires not only continuous improvement systems, but it also requires also customer service to gather feedback from those encountering problems with technology. When users report problems with technology your organization utilizes, be sure to solicit their feedback and follow up in a timely manner to make sure the problem has been resolved. Collect this kind of feedback in a database to track recurring issues. This kind of approach to continuous improvement quickly eliminates ineffective technology and elevates your organization's performance.

BALANCING IT ALL

TAKE CARE OF YOURSELF

In navigating the busyness of your world, ensure you have time for God, your family, and yourself. I learned early in life, as a member of the Sunlight Girl's Club, that I needed to respect myself, because I was *somebody*. In later years, I decided respecting myself meant taking time for myself. As a young working mother, priorities included time not only for family, friends, and God—but also for me. This meant time to rest, relax, and meditate, as well as time to do those things in life I most enjoyed. While carving out such time proves challenging to this very day, it remains a steadfast goal. I have found that when I do these things, I have more energy and peace as I deal with daily challenges and opportunities. Here are steps I have taken to integrate self-care into my routine.

- **Laugh and smile often.** *Try to keep from taking yourself and your work too seriously. Take moments to look around and enjoy all the beauty that surrounds you. Remember that tomorrow is never promised.*

- **Make time for your passions.** *Dancing is one of my favorite activities. Not only have I taken swing dancing lessons, but I have also made dancing part of my exercise plan.*

- **Pay attention to your health.** *Develop a pro-active plan that includes healthy eating, exercise, and adequate sleep. Use prayer and meditation to reduce stress. Consult doctors, nutritionists, and other professionals. Explore natural and wholistic approaches to wellness.*

- **Take time away from the technology.** *Tell co-workers how to reach you in an emergency. Then, turn off e-mail, text, and other technologies as you spend personal time away for work. Instead, focus on the people and events around you.*

- **Plan a make-up day.** *Plan a day on your calendar to preform important tasks you have been unable to complete. In a similar manner, consider setting aside a day for your family to address important matters that might have flown under the radar for far too long. Utilize vacation time or personal days, if needed.*

- **Protect family time**. *Remember to include parents, in-laws, your spouse, children, and grandchildren. Schedule time on the calendar for extended times together at the beginning of each year.*

- **Cook one time each week.** *Plan a week's menu for your family and cook once for the entire week. Additionally, cook some foods in large quantities to freeze them for later use. Both methods save time. By preparing several meats, vegetables, and sides at once, your family will have many choices throughout the week. In my family, this is a valuable Sunday tradition.*

- **Schedule weekly family date nights.** *Many jobs can become all-consuming, causing family relationships to suffer. Plan deliberate time to spend with important family members. Ask your staff to avoid scheduling commitments on these nights, but make sure they know how to reach you in an emergency.*

KNOW YOUR LIFE'S PURPOSE

A nswer this essential question for yourself: *What is God's purpose for my life and how does it connect to my work at home, at my job, and in my community?* For me, it has taken years to arrive at a complete answer. Doug Sherman and William D. Hendricks's *Your Work Matters to God* first helped me wrestle with this matter.[8] Later, a personal strengths inventory revealed empathy, administration, and leadership as my primary spiritual gifts. Over the years, I have come to realize that my life's purpose is to use my gifts of empathy and leadership to recognize and respond to the needs of those around me, leading efforts to address the struggles I see. In short, my mission is to serve the people God places in my path. Sometimes, this results in leading large national efforts, and other times it means guiding smaller efforts to assist the people I live and learn with each day. To ensure I keep my life's purpose central to all my work, each year I develop a mission statement for my career and a vision statement about my future. From these, I create spiritual goals and an action plan for each new year. Journaling about my efforts every month also allows me to reflect on my progress. This process keeps me focused on living according to my life's purpose.

FINAL REFLECTION

Life is a journey. Listening to God and your fellow travelers crafts meaning from experiences along the way. After some time, your own voice will emerge from their words which will still echo in your mind. Then, you can speak into the lives of those who trek beside you on the path, sharing a piece of the truths and the souls that came before you. In this way, the legacy continues as each person adds their voice to the eternal exchange. People, families, nations—and truly the world— become richer as we each share the best of our own learning. Strong leaders take the time to share lessons learned, as they engage in mentoring generations of future leaders. Our united voices wind an unending golden thread between the ones who walk ahead of and behind us on life's journey.

I am honored to have learned from some of the greatest minds this world has to offer. I am humbled by the opportunity to add my voice to theirs. Indeed, the conversation continues as we hold true to the biblical principle that older men and women—through their lives, words, and actions—must shape the next generation (Titus 2:3-5).

The circle of learning and growing continues, both as we learn from others and share our learning with others. Future generations are counting on us to share, as we guide them to achieve their goals and together develop a nation and world that we are all proud to leave for our children and grandchildren.

AFTERWORD

Legacy. This practice of one generation sharing with the next is a vital concept. As a Millennial, it is meaningful to me as I consider my present role as an emerging leader and as I look forward to raising a family of my own. But it is in looking back on my childhood that I find the clearest shining examples of legacy. For example, my parents shared their unconditional love. They provided for my physical needs—like food and shelter—without asking for anything in return. They didn't ask for money to cover the meals they fed me, and they didn't invoice me for childhood missteps that led to broken windows and furniture. They shared with me freely. This included sharing wisdom from their own life experiences. Their unconditional love and shared wisdom are their enduring legacy to me. My life was built on the foundation of my parents' legacy, but that was only the beginning.

We've all heard that it takes a village to raise a child. Indeed, every child depends on the elders around them to cultivate a strong, healthy village. But what does it take for a village to turn a child into a productive citizen? That only happens when the village leaders take time to shape the next generation into successful leaders. In response, the next generation must listen carefully to village leaders who selflessly invest in them. Beyond just listening, they must appropriately apply the lessons learned from those who have gone before them. In this way, wisdom of the ages echoes through the generations.

Dr. Jennifer Wimbish has been a stalwart member of a village committed to my success since I met her years earlier, as a child in Jack and Jill of America, Incorporated. Today, in pondering deeply which gifts of legacy most impacted me, I am grateful for those like Dr. Wimbish who write about encounters that were pivotal to their success. How else will those who come behind them learn the unique truths that launched them into excellence? And how else can I thank my village except by building on the bold, honest lessons collected through their experiences and similarly shared in books like Dr. Wimbish's? The blueprints provided in *Leadership Lessons for All Generations* compel me to build on these lessons as I form new villages and leave my own legacy for coming generations. I invite you join me in this work of legacy—whether you are a Millennial like me or a member of some other generation—and I welcome your village to partner with mine.

Respectfully,
Nicholas Lipscomb
Jack and Jill of America Incorporated
Alumni, Mentee, and Mentor

> "My mission in life is not merely to survive, but to thrive;
> and to do so with some passion, some compassion,
> some humor, and some style."
>
> —Maya Angelou

NOTES

NOTES

NOTES

CONTRIBUTING TO THE CONVERSATION:

PLANNING WORKSHEETS

What you do today can improve all tomorrows.

— Ralph Marston

L
ife is a journey, where learning occurs from those special individuals and mentors God has placed in our path. Additionally, our spiritual journey includes God speaking to us in many different ways. Someone once said that each of us is placed in a special location with special people, engineered by God, so that we become the individual that he would have us to be. It is important for each of us to take some time to reflect on that learning, sharing critical life changing words with others as appropriate and ordered by God.[9]

Upon reflection, what words of wisdom from this material do you want to integrate into your lifestyle? What actions will you take to have this occur?

LESSONS LEARNED FROM THE BOOK THAT I PLAN TO INTEGRATE INTO MY LIFESTYLE:

1. _____
_____
_____
_____

Outcome Desired: _____
_____

2. _____
_____
_____
_____

Outcome Desired: _____
_____

3. _____
_____
_____
_____

Outcome Desired: _____
_____

4. _____

_____

_____

_____

Outcome Desired: _____

_____

5. _____

_____

_____

_____

Outcome Desired: _____

_____

ACTIONS TO TAKE AND TIMELINE

Should correspond with the numbered list above.

ACTIONS	COMPLETION DATE	EVALUATION (✓)

IN YOUR OWN PERSONAL VOICE

What words of wisdom would you share with others?

1. _____
   _____
   _____
   _____
   _____
   _____
   _____

2. _____
   _____
   _____
   _____
   _____
   _____
   _____

3. _____
   _____
   _____
   _____
   _____
   _____

ENDNOTES

1. Hilliard, Seretha Butler. The Consummate Teacher: "An African American Woman." Kearney, NE: Morris Publishing, 2002.
2. Garcia, Laura. "Sunlight Girls Club Presented Historical Marker." Victoria Advocate, July 15, 2015. Accessed June 27, 2018. https://www.victoriaadvocate.com/news/education/sunlight-girls-club-presented-with-historical-marker/article_d8acbefe-bea4-570d-8a36-618834224c81.html.
3. Akers, Doris. You Can't Beat God Giving (Recorded by Sky Pilot Choir with the Sutton Sisters). On The Sky Pilot Choir Vol. 2 [Album]. Reseda, California: Christian Faith Recording, 1957. http://Website URL.
4. Rodriguez, Richard. Hunger of Memory: The Education of Richard Rodriguez. New York, NY: Dial Press/ Random House, 1982.
5. Langford International, Inc. "Langford Learning: Improving the Quality of Learning and Leading - An Overview Booklet." LangfordLearning.com. 2014. http://www.langfordlearning.com/resource/Langford-Learning.pdf.
6. Sarrat, Olivier. "The Five Whys Technique." Cornell University IRL School. 2010. Accessed June 27, 2018. https://digitalcommons.ilr.cornell.edu/cgi/viewcontent.cgi?article=1200&context=intl.
7. See "Decision Making Strategy" – "The World of Decision Making Explained." Decision Making Confidence. Accessed June 27, 2018. https://www.decision-making-confidence.com/.
8. Sherman, Doug, and William D. Hendricks. Your Work Matters to God. Colorado Springs, CO: NavPress, 1990.
9. See: Warren, Richard. The Purpose Driven Life: What on Earth Am I Here For? Grand Rapids, MI: Zondervan, 2002.

REFERENCES

Akers, Doris. You Can't Beat God Giving (Recorded by Sky Pilot Choir with the Sutton Sisters). On The Sky Pilot Choir Vol. 2 [Album]. Reseda, California: Christian Faith Recording, 1957.

"Decision making strategy" - "The World of Decision Making Explained." Decision Making Confidence. Accessed June 27, 2018. https://www. decision-making-confidence.com/.

Garcia, Laura. "Sunlight Girls Club Presented Historical Marker." Victoria Advocate, July 15, 2015. Accessed June 27, 2018. https://www.victoriaad-vocate.com/news/education/sunlight-girls-club-presented-with-historica l-marker/article_d8acbefe-bea4-570d-8a36-618834224c81.html.

Hilliard, Seretha Butler. The Consummate Teacher: "An African American Woman." Kearney, NE: Morris Publishing, 2002.

Langford International, Inc. "Langford Learning: Improving the Quality of Learning and Leading - An Overview Booklet." LangfordLearning.com. 2014. http://www.langfordlearning.com/resource/Langford-Learning.pdf.

Rodriguez, Richard. Hunger of Memory: The Education of Richard Rodriguez. New York, NY: Dial Press/ Random House, 1982.

Sarrat, Olivier. "The Five Whys Technique." Cornell University IRL School. 2010. Accessed June 27, 2018. https://digitalcommons.ilr.cornell.edu/ cgi/viewcontent.cgi?article=1200&context=intl.

Sherman, Doug, and William D. Hendricks. Your Work Matters to God. Colorado Springs, CO: NavPress, 1990.

Warren, Richard. The Purpose Driven Life: What on Earth Am I Here For? Grand Rapids, MI: Zondervan, 200

ABOUT THE AUTHOR

Dr. Jennifer Wimbish, President Emeritus of Cedar Valley College (CVC), was the first African American President of the College. She is the CEO of BW Success Strategies, Incorporated, a consulting firm focused on strategic planning, success coaching, and solutions connected to problem-solving. Her leadership journey has included her serving as Provost and Chief Academic Officer at Lansing Community College in Michigan; Dean of Students and faculty counselor at Brookhaven College in the Dallas, Texas area; and teacher and counselor within the public school system of Corpus Christi, Texas. Dr. Wimbish has designed and taught leadership courses, presented at leadership conferences across the nation, and published a guide to student leadership. She is a mentor for individuals aspiring to become college presidents, and she is active within her church's outreach and workforce programs.

Since her teenage years, Dr. Wimbish has been engaged in various leadership roles. She founded an organization in Corpus Christi, Texas that engages the community in activities regarding historical, cultural, and equity awareness. This organization still exists today. While in Michigan, she was instrumental in uniting organizations to both develop transitional housing for homeless families and increase access to technology for certain populations. Dr. Wimbish also engineered a partnership with a local Michigan board that resulted in a center for regional employment and training needs.

Jennifer Wimbish's leadership at CVC impacted the lives of many. She led the college to recognition as a military friendly campus, as well as a national model for sustainability. During her tenure, record increases in enrollment, completion, and graduation rates afforded many students access to college. The college's Phi Theta Kappa Chapter won the title of Most Distinguished chapter in the world, contributing to Wimbish receiving their prestigious Michael Bennett Lifetime Achievement Award. Wimbish's dynamic leadership has been acknowledged through such awards as the St. John's (Michigan) Community Unity Award for community collaborations, the National Role Model Award from Minority Access, Inc., and the Woman of the Year Award from the Dallas Women's Council.

Wimbish holds a doctorate degree in higher, adult, and lifelong education from Michigan State University; a master's degree in guidance and counseling from Texas A&M University-Kingsville; and a bachelor's degree in history education from Hampton University (VA).